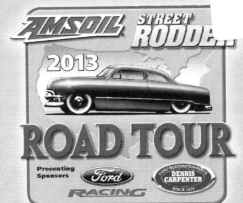

STREET RODDER MAGAZINE

GUIDE TO BUILDING A '51 FORD

HOT ROD NETWORK
STREET ROD GROUP

STREET ROD GROUP DIRECTOR
Brian Brennan

SENIOR TECH EDITOR
Ron Ceridono

WRITTEN BY
Brian Brennan, Gerry Burger, Tommy Lee
Byrd, Ron Ceridono, and Stephen Kim

PHOTOGRAPHY BY
Gerry Burger, Tommy Lee Byrd,
Ron Ceridono, Stephen Kim, Robert
McGaffin, and Chuck Vranas

ART DIRECTOR
Michael Stanford

COPY EDITOR
Sarah Gonzales

EVP/GROUP PUBLISHER
Doug Evans

GROUP PUBLISHER
Tim Foss

ASSOCIATE PUBLISHER
Janeen Webb

GROUP PUBLISHER'S ASSISTANT
Yasmin Fajatin

VP, HOT ROD NETWORK
David Freiburger

GROUP ART DIRECTOR
Markas Platt

ROAD TOUR DIRECTOR
Jerry Dixey

ISBN: 978-1-935231-31-8
© 2014 Source Interlink Magazines, LLC

Contents

CHAPTER 1   06
Meet the Builders of the 2013 AMSOIL/
STREET RODDER Road Tour '51 Ford:
Honest Charley Garage

CHAPTER 2   10
Shoebox Trends: The New Post-War Fords

CHAPTER 3   16
Framing: Fatman Fabrications Provides
the Perfect Platform

CHAPTER 4   26
Combining Tradition and Technology:
High-Tech Running Gear

CHAPTER 5   38
Brakes: Four-Wheel Discs

CHAPTER 6   50
Fighting the Rust Monster:
Making Our Shoebox Whole Again

CHAPTER 7   62
Channeling: Dropping the Shoebox Ford
Over the Frame Without Cutting the Floor

CHAPTER 8   70
Lowering a Shoebox Lid:
The Road Tour Car Goes Low Profile

CHAPTER 9   86
All That Glitters:
Flawless Paint and Brilliant Chrome

CHAPTER 10   98
Support System: Cooling, Plumbing, and Exhaust

CHAPTER 11   116
Comforts for the Road Tour Car:
Electrical, A/C, and Interior

CHAPTER 12   130
Final Details: Finishing the '51 Ford

CHAPTER 13   168
Golden Dream:
The '51 Ford Road Tour Custom Combines
Plenty of Old-Time Kool With Today's Technology

CHAPTER 14   180
Sponsor Information

Meet the Builders of the 2013 AMSOIL/*STREET RODDER* Road Tour '51 Ford — Honest Charley Speed Shop: Then and Now

✳ *BY TOMMY LEE BYRD* ✳ *PHOTOGRAPHY BY THE AUTHOR* ✳

❯ *Honest Charley Speed Shop is alive and well. It's now located within the Coker Tire Complex in historic downtown Chattanooga.*

Decades before anyone had envisioned the vast infrastructure of today's automotive aftermarket, the foundations for all that would develop were taking shape in the mind of one of hot rodding's most imaginative figures, "Honest" Charley Card.

More than just a marketing innovator, Honest Charley was an enthusiast who gained an understanding of all things mechanical early on, eventually keeping his father's fleet of vegetable delivery trucks up and running at a young age. Before his 17th birthday, Charley had purchased a used 1919 Model T touring car, and from there he moved onto a Whippet. Unsatisfied with its original appearance, he began modifying that roadster one part at a time, efforts that were soon recognized by others in and around Chattanooga who wanted their cars to stand out as well.

It was about this same time that local point-to-point races attracted famed racers of the day, including Cannonball Baker, who came to rely on Charley's skills with a wrench. As fortune would have it, Baker's well-tuned Franklin Airman sedan won the celebrated race from downtown Chattanooga to nearby Lookout Mountain in 1928 with a time of 17 minutes and 2 seconds. From then on Baker greeted Charley with a rousing

❱ Here's Honest Charley "Hisself" with his streamlined '39 Ford on the sands of Daytona Beach.

"seventeen oh-two" whenever they met, be it in Daytona Beach, Florida, or at other venues, including continual visits to the Indianapolis 500 that began in 1933.

Following World War II, Charley revived his relationships with notable heroes at the Brickyard and other venues before taking on record attempts of his own. Having initialized development of a 16-valve Model T cylinder head years before, Charley eagerly teamed with Buck Jacks in building a 21-stud Flathead V-8 for use in his channeled '34 Ford Tudor sedan. With the original fenders replaced with his own streamlined fairings, Charley made some initial runs on the hardened sands of Daytona before handing over the wheel to Walt Hartman who managed a respectable 115.6-mph run.

With that achievement, Charley truly understood America's new passion for hot rodding, as well as the need for a reliable source for components that would enable bootleggers, lawmen, hot rodders, and racers to realize their dreams. Born from these simple beginnings in the heart of Chattanooga, Honest Charley Speed Shop opened its doors in 1948, quickly growing to become the first international mail-order speed shop and the most recognized name in the industry.

Incorporating a clever range of homespun marketing methods, it wasn't long before the company's sales network attracted customers from across the nation and around the globe. Displaying his comical artwork, Honest Charley catalogs quickly grew with an ever-expanding array of components from every major manufacturer in the business. While Honest Charley retail stores and distribution centers found their way across Tennessee, Georgia, and Florida, the bulk of the company's sales volume came by way of the now-familiar catalog displaying well-known cartoon caricatures and slogans created by "Honest Hisself." Gems like, "Is your hot rod hot or not?", "Send money, I'll pay the postage," and "Your money back if it ain't right!" Later came others like, "Anyone who answers knows the answer," and of course, "You can't brag if you lag!" that worked their way into the rodding vernacular.

Never far from his involvement with racing, Charley's next endeavor involved a progressively modified '39 Ford that forever became the vehicle he was known by. Sporting an aerodynamic nose with fully enclosed wheels, the channeled sedan was fitted with a bored and stroked Mercury 59A flathead used in record attempts at Daytona,

❱ *The talented crew of Honest Charley Garage was responsible for the construction of the 2013 AMSOIL/STREET RODDER Road Tour '51 Ford. (Left to right, near side of the car): Toby Quinton, Jonathan Sullivan, Jonathan Myren, and Richard Marter. (Left to right, far side of the car): Ben Langston, Ben Giuliano, Greg Cunningham, Greg Mills, Delton Scott, Keith Brown, and Hal Everrett.*

eventually reaching 137 mph in 1953. Despite other attempts in its class this record was never exceeded.

By then Charley and his wife, Gracie, who had been running their own restaurant and a delicatessen in addition to their speed shop, decided it was all too much and got out of the food businesses entirely to devote all of their efforts into further development of their greatest endeavor. As Honest Charley's following grew in step with the industry over time, it's widely acknowledged that other fledgling speed shops applied Honest Charley's collective marketing techniques to their catalogs, again proving that "imitation is the best form of flattery!" As the company grew, so too did their accommodations in and around Chattanooga and with that growth came a succession of notable staff members, including a youngster named Mike Goodman.

Having served our nation with honor as a United States Marine in Vietnam, Goodman returned to his lifelong involvement with hot rods, building a succession of cars, including a homebuilt T-bucket that he drove to the second NSRA Nationals in 1971 and many thereafter. Later, he became one of Honest Charley's valued staff members, eventually earning his position as national

sales manager for Honest Charley Speed Distributors Warehouse. In the years that followed, the company evolved and in 1990 Honest Charley Speed Shop took a time-out. Then, in 1998, Chattanooga businessman and entrepreneur Corky Coker and enthusiast Mike Goodman secured the trademarks and began aggressively rebuilding the Honest Charley brand. Those who know Mr. Goodman will certainly affirm that his affable nature and thorough understanding of the needs and hopes of hot rodders everywhere has allowed the dream to live on, just as "Honest Hisself" would want it to be.

As the second inductee into the Specialty Equipment Market Association (SEMA) Hall of Fame in 1970, it goes without saying that hot rodding acknowledges a debt of gratitude to Honest Charley Card for innovations that helped in the formation of our industry and a lifestyle that is so cherished today. Now, more than ever, Honest Charley Speed Shop reminds us of what once was and how we can celebrate the liberties that our great nation has to offer.

Today, Honest Charley Speed Shop continues its rise to international prominence as one of the Coker companies, thanks to the tireless efforts of Corky Coker and Mike

❱ Mike Goodman began working for the original Honest Charley Speed Shop and today he's bringing his expertise to its revival. That's Goodman with his T-bucket in a snapshot dated September 1972.

❱ The showroom of the new Honest Charley Speed Shop. The parts are new but the same old commitment to customer satisfaction of the original remains.

Goodman, two true car enthusiasts providing classic hot rod components to enthusiasts around the globe. In addition to the Speed Shop, the Honest Charley name has grown into a hot rod and restoration shop, known as Honest Charley Garage. From simple repairs to high-end restorations, Honest Charley Garage is equipped with a number of skilled craftsmen, led by Greg Cunningham. Many Honest Charley Garage builds have received national recognition, but one of the most eye-catching builds to date is the 2013 AMSOIL/*STREET RODDER* Road Tour car, a beautiful '51 Ford custom. Other notable builds include a number of cool cars from Corky Coker's up-and-coming TV show.

Undoubtedly, the Honest Charley legacy is being held high, even after 65 years of business. With the new Speed Shop staff, and the addition of Honest Charley Garage, you're likely to hear a lot more about Honest Charley in the near future.

The New Postwar Fords

✳ *BY RON CERIDONO* ✳ *PHOTOGRAPHY BY THE AUTHOR, CHUCK VRANAS, AND GERRY BURGER* ✳

❯ *This ground-hugging '49 Ford Club Coupe has been nosed, decked, and fitted with frenched headlights. In the Ford series the Club Coupe sold slightly over 4,000 while the Business coupe had over 29,000 sales (the Business Coupe had fixed rear windows, they opened on the Club Coupe). The Custom Club Coupe was the third best-selling model in 1949, selling over 150,000.*

Ith the conclusion of World War II Americans gave a collective sigh of relief and began looking forward to life without shortages and rationing. Due to the demand for raw materials needed for the war effort, production of civilian automobiles came to a halt on February 10, 1942. As a result, very few new vehicles were available that year, so by 1946 the public was anxious to buy the cars that were slowly beginning to appear in the nation's showrooms. But while these new cars were fresh off the assembly line there wasn't very much that was new. They were the same old pre-war models from four years before with minor changes.

Ford resumed automobile production when the war was over but the company was in serious trouble and things quickly got worse. By 1946 losses were said to be in the tens of millions of dollars per month. Ford's troubles had been a while in the making—Edsel Ford had become president of the automotive empire in 1919 but Henry Ford, his father and founder of the company, remained the power behind the throne. Henry

and Edsel's relationship was always tumultuous and the elder Ford often blocked his son's attempts to streamline operations and modernize their products. After Henry suffered a series of strokes in the late '30s the man who many considered to be a genius began to exhibit impaired physical abilities and his mental state often came into question.

Edsel Ford was only 49 when he died May 26, 1943, from complications

❯ *The '49 convertible was only available in custom trim but could be ordered with a six-cylinder or V-8 (a 6 or an 8 on the grille's center spinner indicated which engine was under the hood). The convertibles (and the wagons) used frames with X-members similar to the '48 and earlier cars for increased strength. The ragtops had leather interiors and sales of over 50,000.*

after stomach cancer surgery so Henry, despite his health issues, became the president of the company once more. At the time Ford Motor Company was heavily involved in war production, building B-24 Liberator bombers, aircraft engines, Jeeps, and other vehicles, including gliders. Because of the company's importance to the war effort, and Henry's deteriorating condition, the government kept a close eye on him and it has been reported that contingency plans to manage the company if he was no longer up to the task were proposed. Henry's overall condition continued to deteriorate and in September of 1945 Edsel's eldest son, Henry Ford II, took the reins of the company. Henry died April 7, 1947, at the age of 83.

At the age of 28 Henry Ford II (often referred to as HFII, or Hank the Deuce) found himself faced with the task of rebuilding the company. When civilian automobile production resumed in July of 1945 Ford cars were still riding on solid axles and transverse spring suspension that began with the Model T. Although the Flathead V-8 received some updates, the same old transmission, enclosed driveline, and banjo rearend were still being used. Styling wasn't any more inspired as all the "new models" were warmed-over 1942 designs. The real problem was Ford lacked the engineering and design staffs to make any significant changes of any sort. HFII met that challenge by doing the obvious, he hired some of the best people in the industry—many of whom were working for or had worked for the competition, namely General Motors. Among others he brought in Ernest Breech, formerly of GM's Bendix Division, Harold Youngren who had once been Oldsmobile's chief engineer, and a stylist named George Walker.

It took a revitalized staff and a huge investment in revised production facilities and in 1949 the all-new Ford was introduced. Ford's marketing campaign was brilliant. At first the new car was kept top secret, which served to make the press and public curious. Then there were "leaked" announcements that cranked up the rumor mill and finally came the debut and public showing of the car. Ford gave the new '49 Ford a lavish introduction at New York's Waldorf Astoria on June 10, 1948, well ahead of the competition's dates for revealing their new cars.

Like its predecessor the '49 Fords were still powered by either a Flathead V-8 (which had received a number of improvements) or inline-six, and the wheelbase remained the same at 114 inches—but virtually everything else was redesigned. There was a new, lighter ladder frame (the convertible and station wagon had the earlier style X-member for added strength) with coil spring–equipped independent front suspension, in the rear was a Hotchkiss-style axle on longitudinal leaf springs, and tubular shock absorbers were used on both ends. The brakes and steering were improved and the new cars were lighter.

The most obvious difference in the new Fords was the sleek new slab-sided styling. The hood was broad and flowed into the fenders, the grille was modern looking with a hint of "jet age" styling, the slab sides were smooth with no signs of fenders, and the taillights were integrated into the rear fins with subdued wind splits. Fords were stylish, tasteful, and totally different than what the company had offered previously.

For 1949 there were two trim levels, one was simply referred to as a Ford and was available as a two-door sedan, four-door sedan (referred to a Tudor and Fordor),

❱ This '49 convertible has a hood full of louvers and wears one of the "bullnose" trim pieces that replaced the stock hood ornament. Twin spotlights are another vintage touch, as are the Cad hubcaps with spinners. Another cool custom touch—the stock door handles have been exchanged for Lincoln push buttons.

six-passenger Club Coupe, and three-passenger Business Coupe. The upscale trim line was designated the Custom series, it included two- and four-door sedans, six-passenger Club Coupe, convertible, and the new wood-clad, metal-framed station wagon.

With the success of the '49 Ford not much needed changing, nonetheless for the following year one of the ad slogans announced there were "50 changes for 1950." Some of the noticeable updates included a new hood ornament, the grille bar now wrapped around the front fenders, and the parking lights were relocated below the grille. The gas filler was hidden behind a flap in the left rear fender, and the doors were now opened with push buttons in the handles. Some of the other changes, like a new horn ring, weren't as noticeable.

There were also model changes for 1950. What had been referred to as the Ford was now called the DeLuxe and the Custom series became the Custom DeLuxe. The only body styles available in DeLuxe trim were the two- and four-door sedans and the Business Coupe. Custom DeLuxe versions include the Tudor and Fordor, Club Coupe, station wagon, convertible, and later in the year the Crestliner. Designed to compete with the hardtops offered by GM and Chrysler, the Crestliner was based on the Tudor sedan. Only available in green or maroon, special side trim with black inserts was part of the package, along with a vinyl top, fender skirts, special hubcaps, and unique interior features, including a special steering wheel.

For 1951, Fords had a new look, despite the fact that the same basic body was still used. The two trim series were now referred to as DeLuxe for the base models and Custom for the upscale models. Up front all series were treated to a redesigned grille with twin "spinners" (or jet intakes, depending on who was describing them) rather than the single seen the previous two years. The new

frontend treatment included a new hood. In the rear there were larger taillights and inside the instrument panel was redesigned. But the big news for 1951 was the introduction of the Victoria hardtop. This was also the first year for the Ford-O-Matic automatic transmission.

To say the '49, '50, and '51 Fords were a success is an understatement—they saved the company with production of roughly 3 million cars during those three years. Judging by their popularity today, they are still a success as the reception of the AMSOIL/*STREET RODDER* '51 Ford Road Tour car has received proves.

SHOEBOXES OF ALL SORTS

Thanks to the slab-sided and rectangular shape of the '49-51 Fords they quickly picked up the nickname "shoebox" to distinguish them for their fat-fendered predecessors. Call them what you will, they make great street rods.

Here are some of our favorite examples:

❭ *The wagons had some unique features: the rear windows slid to open, the spare tire was carried at the rear under a metal cover, and the unique taillights had a rod and hinge arrangement that made them rotate so they could still be seen with the tailgate down.*

❭ *Once sought after by surfers, street rodders covet Ford wagons as well. This '49 has been smoothed all around and has a smoothed and tucked front bumper. Notice the contrast between the redesigned station wagon body with the '46 Ford in the background. Among many other differences, the '49 had a steel roof with a headliner; the earlier body was all wood with a cloth top.*

❭ *Ford's station wagon for 1949 was now a two-door and used a steel body with wood panels that were no longer structural. As in years past, the woodwork was created and installed at the Iron Mountain plant in Michigan. The most expensive model in 1949, the station wagon carried a price tag of $2,264 with a V-8 ($2,119 with the six). Available in custom trim only, over 31,000 were sold.*

❯ This clean '50 is a Custom DeLuxe six-passenger Club Coupe. Selling over 85,000 they carried a $1,595 price tag with a V-8, the six-cylinder version was slightly less at $1,511. Note the grille bar now extends around the fenders and parking lights have been relocated. Here again a bullnose replaces the original hood ornament—in the '50s it was a cheap alternative to having the hood nosed at a body shop.

❯ Ranking third in sales for 1950 was the Custom DeLuxe Fordor with more than 240,000 sold. The Custom DeLuxe versions had stainless trim around the windshield and rear window that the DeLuxe series lacked. Interestingly on Custom DeLuxe cars the side trim just in front of the doors read Ford Custom rather than Custom DeLuxe; the trim on the DeLuxe series was plain.

❯ Although all '50 convertibles were Custom DeLuxe series, this one lacks the identifying trim on the front fenders, nonetheless it's still a great looking car. Ford convertibles outsold Chevrolets this year by a considerable margin. Sales and production numbers don't always agree for a variety of reasons, but the most reliable sources indicate the difference in sales was near 20,000 cars.

❯ New for 1951 were the redesigned grille, hood, and round parking lights. Possibly owing to the introduction of the hardtop, convertible sales dipped to slightly under 41,000. Priced at $1,949 the only engine available was the Flathead V-8. This one has been nosed and the painted headlight rings almost make the lights look frenched.

❯ Another '51 convertible, this one has been chopped and also features other subtle modifications. Nosed and decked, the door handles have been removed, front fenders have been extended, and the headlights frenched. Shortened side trim and wide whites on chrome wheels are nice old-school touches.

❱ *Proving that these cars don't need lots of modifications to be cool is this custom series Club Coupe. Although the hood ornament has been removed the Ford crest remains. Note the V-8 emblem on the fender in front of the door—six-cylinder cars had plain fenders with no engine identification. Slightly over 53,000 were sold for $1,590; six-cylinder cars were $85 less.*

❱ *Introduced in late 1951 was the Victoria two-door hardtop. Sales exceeded 110,000 and despite the late introduction the Victoria outsold Chevrolet's Bel Air that came to market two years earlier. At $1,925 the Victoria was only a few dollars less than the convertible at $1,949.*

❱ *Often misidentified as a coupe, this is a DeLuxe Tudor sedan with a V-8. These plain Jane models, which were third in sales for the year, lacked the full-length side trim found on the custom versions, which was Ford's top seller for the year. Prices were $1,492 and $1,585, respectively.*

❱ *The one-piece windshield and side glass give this '51 Tudor a unique look. Note the unique side trim and the scoop behind the front wheel—all the work of someone who knows how to use an airbrush.*

❱ *Mild customizing tricks work well on shoebox Fords as this example shows. De-chromed from end to end, the door handles and all the other barbs have been eliminated, which results in a very smooth, and in this case, very low, ride.*

❱ Shoebox Fords were also given the full-on custom treatment. Valley Custom worked over Ron Dunn's '50 Ford not once, but twice. First time around was in 1953; a second round took place after the car was hit in 1957.

❱ A popular change to '51s was the substitution of a straight grille bar that was available in the '50s from a variety of sources, including Honest Charley "hisself."

❱ A much more serious modification was sectioning, or taking a strip of metal out of the body and then welding it back together. Not for the timid, a number of well-known Shoebox customs were sectioned but not chopped.

❱ One of the most well known customs from the '50s is Ron Courtney's X-51. The 5-inch section and the huge fins on the owner designed and built '51 created quite a stir when introduced in 1958. Courtney installed a 265 Chevy with a McCulloch supercharger.

❱ A tastefully done example of a contemporary custom Shoebox is Lee Pratt's '49 Club Coupe. Those are real Appleton spotlights and the side trim is '55 Chevy, upside down. There's still a Flathead under the hood.

Fatman Fabrications Provides the Perfect Platform

✳ BY GERRY BURGER ✳ PHOTOGRAPHY BY THE AUTHOR ✳

❯ *Every Fatman Fabrications chassis is fabricated in a dedicated frame fixture and painstakingly assembled to ensure the highest quality.*

I t wasn't that long ago that reproduction framerails for '30s-era cars were considered exotic stuff, and then came the complete reproduction chassis. Fatman Fabrications was around to see and help lead all of this progress and today they produce a wide array of complete frames for cars from the '30s through the late '50s. When you combine the complete chassis lineup with their extensive line of front clips for cars there aren't many vehicles from the '30s to '60s that can't be fitted with a good set of Fatman suspenders.

With that long history of building a quality chassis that will handle thousands of miles of road service, Fatman Fabrications was the natural choice for supplying the chassis for the 2013 AMSOIL/*STREET RODDER* Road Tour car.

Due to the time constraints on getting the '51 Ford completely built at Honest Charley Garage, Brent Vandervort was kind enough to send his display chassis down to Chattanooga right after the NSRA Street Rod Nationals. OK, it was wearing bright yellow display paint but at least we had a complete chassis to begin the build.

Of course looking at a finished chassis is one thing, but getting up close and personal during the complete fabrication of the chassis is the only way to truly appreciate the time, material, and craftsmanship that goes into each and every Fatman Fabrications chassis.

Fatman Fabrications offers a broad range of suspension options, all based on the ever-popular Mustang II style of front suspension. They can build the frame from a basic and budget-minded coil spring front and leaf spring rear, to the more exotic pro touring style of chassis with coilover suspension on all four corners, beefy antisway bars, and big Wilwood brakes. Stainless steel four-links or mild steel are another option so you

❱ The chassis is built from sub-assemblies that are prefabricated before finding their way to the frame fixture.

❱ Many of the Fatman Fabrications chassis and suspension frame stubs share the same front crossmember so they are always producing the items from heavy wall rectangular tubing.

❱ The pre-formed parts are neatly stacked awaiting assembly. This saves production time since all the parts are on hand prior to actual chassis construction.

❱ The cutouts in the crossmember have now been filled with plate, tack-welded in place, and are ready for final welding. The notches provide engine clearance and rack-and-pinion clearance.

can truly have your chassis built to reflect your exact needs. Fatman also offers a stepped rear frame for those who prefer to roll around on wide rear rubber. Complete brake line installation is another option and when you see how neat the lines are run you'll be checking that box off too. The options are yours and there is a package to fit most budgets.

We opted for QA1 coilover suspension on all four corners with sway bars front and rear. Big Wilwood brakes will provide the stopping power (more on that when we assemble the suspension) and a new assembly will ensure miles of trouble-free motoring.

The chassis is fabricated in a dedicated frame fixture to ensure every frame fits a '51 Ford, and that means the body mount holes are drilled and ready to accept your original Ford body. Actually building the frame is like assembling a giant puzzle, subsets of parts are prefabricated and then all of the pieces are assembled on the aforementioned frame fixture. Special attention is paid to precise alignment, high-quality welding and a well-finished final product.

We had the pleasure of working with Eric Kisiah during the construction of this chassis and like all of the fabricators at Fatman

Fabrication, his craftsmanship, attention to detail, and welding is all first class. So follow along as we fabricate a brand-new '51 Ford chassis, and as we mentioned before, we'll get into the suspension installation later when the team at Honest Charley Garage fit the EcoBoost V-6 to the Fatman Fabrications frame.

❱ After some welding and grinding the front crossmember looks like it was formed from one piece; craftsmanship is top notch.

❱ The rear crossmember is a complex piece formed from no less than eight pieces and that doesn't include the additional four-link brackets. This piece is assembled in a fixture to ensure perfect alignment.

❱ The bosses that mount the rack-and-pinion to the front of the crossmember are a precise fit and are welded inside the tubing crossmember.

❱ After welding and grinding we have another great looking piece for our frame. The holes in the rear crossmember provide exhaust pipe clearance, while the centersection incorporates a driveshaft loop.

❱ The finished front crossmember is as strong as it is good looking. This piece will mount our power rack-and-pinion unit.

❱ The framerails are fabricated from a series of pre-cut pieces of box tubing; these are the parts of our framerail all cut and ready to go.

❯ Some of the body mounting holes are located on the tubing and cut on the milling machine, and then the other mounts are cut using this reference point, ensuring our '51 Ford will bolt directly to the frame.

❯ The actual assembly of the chassis begins by dropping in the two front pieces of the framerails and clamping them securely to the frame fixture.

❯ Eric Kisiah uses a magnetic drill press to cut the access holes in the side of the framerails. These holes permit access to the pre-drilled body mounting holes.

❯ Alignment tabs are then welded into the vertical sides of the frame section. This plate ensures proper alignment and provides a "penetration plate" in the root of the weld, ensuring a super-strong joint.

❯ The rear kickup section of the frame is fabricated on the bench and will be blended into the main framerails. While we opted for a stock measurement chassis, Fatman can also step these pieces inboard for additional tire clearance.

❯ Prior to making any welds on the framerails both ends of the tubing are chamfered to ensure good penetration of the welds.

❯ Framerail sections continue to be aligned in the fixture and clamped securely. The entire rail is located prior to tack welding any of the joints.

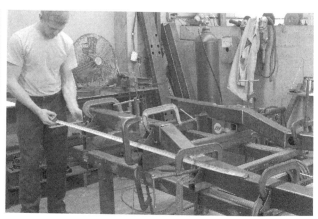

❯ Even though the pieces are clamped in the fixture, measurements are constantly checked prior to welding. Here the distance from the second body mount hole to the front frame end is checked.

❯ This illustrates two things, first there are several complex angles in the side framerails, and second it takes a lot of clamps to hold a framerail together for welding.

❯ Certain that all pieces are in order, the tack welding begins. All the joints are tack welded prior to any complete joint welds.

❯ Centerline posts are built into the frame fixture. From these posts a centerline string is pulled. The string enables the fabricator to take accurate measurements to ensure the 'rails are parallel and true.

❯ One of the tricky spots on the chassis is the transition from the main framerail to the rear kickup. Once again alignment tabs inside the box tubing align the pieces.

❯ A transition piece is formed from a piece of the box tubing to blend the framerails together, here the vertical weld has been completed in the proper up-hill welding pattern. This will all be ground smooth.

❯ All four pieces are now joined at the rear corner of the chassis, once again chamfered joints for strength and perfect alignment are paramount.

❯ The rear crossmember and framerail corner is a complex corner with a lot of machined pieces. This is to provide mounts and access for the stock '51 Ford bumpers.

❯ The corner plates were first tacked in place, and then finished welded to the rear crossmember and side rail. This is a fine example of what a structural weld should look like.

❯ A strong magnetic bar holds the top corner plate in place; note that all body mount holes have been drilled in the rear crossmember, too.

❯ With the perimeter chassis now tack-welded together it is time to locate the front crossmember. All measurements are on a CAD drawing supplied to the fabricator with each chassis order.

❯ The front crossmember is tack welded in place with 3 degrees of antidive built into the placement, which is all part of proper alignment.

❯ The centerpieces that connect the two outer legs of the upper X-member incorporate a driveshaft loop that will clear the stock '51 Ford floor tunnel.

❯ Moving to the center of the chassis X-member construction begins by installing the two upper legs of the X-member. Once again the fixture locates the pieces precisely.

❯ The rear crossmember is then located and tack-welded in place. Once again the center line string serves as a reference to ensure all the crossmembers are in proper alignment.

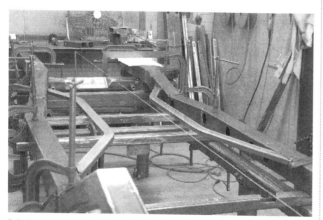

❯ Both upper pieces are tack-welded in place and measurements have been taken from the center line string.

❯ The final crossmember is the coilover shock mount crossmember that rests atop the rear frame kickup sections.

❱ From the front of the chassis looking rearward you can see the complex and strong network of crossmembers that make the Fatman Fabrications chassis super strong.

❱ Once again a few giant C-clamps mate the upper and lower portions of the center X-member.

❱ The frame is now lifted out of the frame fixture with a fork truck. The lower half of the center X-member will be fitted while the chassis is on a frame rotisserie.

❱ With all eight of the lower X-member pieces tacked in place it becomes clear that this is one very rigid platform for the shoebox Ford.

❱ With the frame attached to the chassis rotisserie we are ready to install the bottom side of the center X-member, which is a mirror image of the top section.

❱ The chassis rotisserie makes short work of the finish welding. Alternating sides of the chassis prevent distortion from welding.

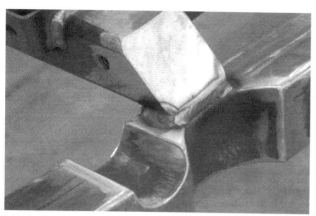

❯ The front crossmember is finish welded adjoining the recess formed for the spring pocket and the C-notch for the rack-and-pinion.

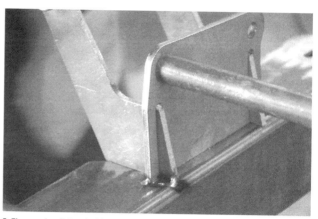

❯ The crossbar fixture holds the two sides in perfect alignment during the welding process; here we have the brackets tack welded in place.

❯ After welding up the entire chassis Eric Kisiah turns his attention to mounting the suspension brackets. Our chassis is using QA1 coilover shocks on all four corners so coilover brackets are installed.

❯ The front coilover brackets are then finish welded, alternating from side to side of the chassis to prevent any chance of chassis distortion.

❯ Note how the coilover upper bracket piece interlocks prior to welding. This makes for one very strong mount. Fatman Fabrications also offers conventional coil spring pockets.

❯ Moving to the rear of the chassis it is time to attach the forward brackets for the rear four-link suspension that will locate the Currie rear. The QA1 shocks mount behind the housing of the rear crossmember.

❯ With the welding complete it is time to dress down the welds with a grinder. After a couple of hours the framerails appear to be one piece.

❯ The finished frame is a fine piece of work; you'll note there are no motor mounts on this chassis as Honest Charley Garage will have to fabricate special mounts for the new EcoBoost Ford V-6.

❯ There were just a few more body mount holes to drill so the magnetic drill press was put to good use once again. Having the body mount holes drilled takes the mystery out of fitting your Ford to the frame.

❯ This side view shows the "outrigger" body mounts in place on the outside of the framerails; this is a true bolt-in chassis.

❯ Fatman Fabrications has been a longtime supporter of the AMSOIL/STREET RODDER Road Tour. Check out this vintage 1998 poster still hanging in the chassis shop.

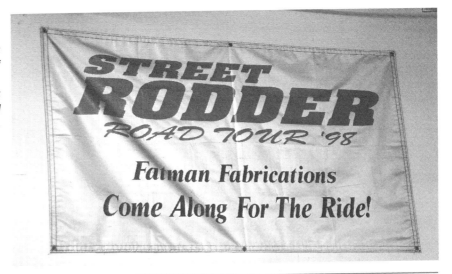

STREET RODDER
ROAD TOUR '98
Fatman Fabrications
Come Along For The Ride!

High-Tech Running Gear

*BY RON CERIDONO * PHOTOGRAPHY BY GERRY BURGER*

❯ *Honest Charley Garage added custom touches to the EcoBoost V-6 on the plenum chamber and cams covers—and look closely and you'll see the Honest Charley "hisself" logo on the oil filler cap.*

Looks can certainly be deceiving and a case in point is the AMSOIL/ *STREET RODDER* Road Tour car for 2013. From its traditional outward appearance it wouldn't be surprising if there was a Flathead powering the car. Even an early Cad or Olds wouldn't be a shock and of course most onlookers would assume that a small-block Chevy or Ford would be found nestled between the fenders. But when the hood is popped on our '51 Ford it's clear that tradition has taken a holiday and in its place is cutting-edge technology in the form of a new twin-turbocharged Ford EcoBoost V-6.

TWIN-TURBO TECH

Based on the Duratec V-6 that has been used in the United States and Europe, the EcoBoost V-6 has a 3.6-inch bore and a 3.41 stroke for 213 ci, or 3,496 cc. In FoMoCo speak, this engine is referred to as the EcoBoost 3.5L GTDI (Gasoline Turbocharged Direct Injection); our example came from Ford Racing Performance Parts and carried PN M-6007-35T.

Some of EcoBoost's noteworthy technical details include:
  365 hp at 5,000 rpm
  420 lb-ft of torque at 2,500 rpm
  All-aluminum construction
  10.0:1 compression ratio
  Dual-overhead camshafts with variable camshaft timing
  High-pressure direct fuel injection
  Regular unleaded fuel recommended
  Lightweight die-cast aluminum block with six-bolt press-fit main bearing caps with piston-cooling jets
  Fully counterweighted forged steel crankshaft

High-strength forged powder metal connecting rods with floating pins

Lightweight aluminum high-strength pistons with low-friction skirt coating

Tuned composite upper and lower intake manifold

Dual water-cooled Honeywell/Garrett GT15 turbochargers

6-quart die-cast aluminum deep sump oil pan

Engine weight is 417 pounds (without accessory drive)

Engine kits include:
Starter
Alternator
Front accessory drive and belt
Air cleaner assembly and ducting
Flexplate/flywheel

One of the EcoBoost's impressive statistics for its displacement is the torque curve, which is a result of the turbochargers. Turbocharged engines are often described as having turbo lag, meaning that it takes time for the turbocharger to "spool up" or get the innards up to sufficient speed to produce boost, so low-end power often suffers. Ford opted for relatively small water-cooled Garrett turbos and while they produce less boost than one large turbo is capable of, in this case less is more. By using a pair of small turbos rather than one big one, turbo lag is virtually eliminated, allowing the engine to feel the effects of boost at lower speeds, which results in increased low-rpm power.

Any engine as high tech as the EcoBoost has a host of sophisticated electronic controls, some of which we needed and many that could be eliminate. To determine what to keep and what to toss Honest Charley's head honcho on this project, Greg Cunningham, turned to the team at Fuel Air Spark Technology (FAST) for help. For over 10 years, FAST has been a leading developer of advanced electronic fuel injection and ignition control technology so Cunningham was confident in their ability to create a system for this particular application. David Page and Brian Reese of FAST put their heads together and figured out what it would take to make our EcoBoost run as it should.

To control the ignition system a FAST Extreme Ignition Module was used. Like many other modern engines, the EcoBoost utilizes signals from crankshaft-triggered devices to control a variety of electronic functions, including ignition. A V-6 fires a spark plug every 120 degrees of crankshaft rotation (a V-8 fires every 90 degrees) and the challenge was to interpret and separate the signals needed to control the coil packs from all the other signals that are generated in a stock application—but they did it.

Operating the fuel injection system is a FAST XFI 2.0 that has the most amazing learning capabilities. Once the system is installed, target air/fuel ratios for idle, cruise, and wide-open throttle are established via the Setup Wizard. When the engine is first started the FAST EFI starts out with basic closed-loop operation, which means ECU is comparing readings from the wideband O2 sensor to the targets that have been set. The ECU then makes corrections by adding or subtracting an amount of fuel to make the target numbers and those from the O2 sensor match. As the car accumulates miles, the computer accumulates more data—it learns to provide the proper air/fuel ratio for each and every situation.

Like most EFI systems the computer relies on a variety of sensors to control air/fuel ratios:

Manifold Absolute Pressure Sensor (MAP): senses load, by reading vacuum and is one of the parameters for adjusting mixture.

❱ *Behind the 365hp EcoBoost V-6 is a PCS Controller and a Ford 6R80 six-speed automatic transmission with double overdrive.*

Coolant Temperature Sensor (CTS): essentially the electronic version of a choke, it tells the computer a richer mixture and fast idle are needed to keep the engine running.

Air Temperature Sensor (ATS): it provides one of the parameters for air/fuel ratio—hotter air requires a leaner mixture/cooler air a richer mixture.

Throttle Position Sensor (TPS): acts like an accelerator pump, and provides the computer with additional information—also used to establish shift points for computer-controlled automatic transmissions.

Idle Air Control (IAC): it controls an air bypass in the throttle body to maintain and adjust idle speed.

SIX SPEEDS AND TWO OVERDRIVES

Behind the EcoBoost V-6 is another departure from what has become the street rod norm, a four-speed automatic overdrive transmission. Gear changes, all six of them, are conducted by a Ford 6R80 automatic with double overdrive and a lockup converter. The original application for our particular transmission was a '12 F-150.

6R80 GEAR RATIOS

As the following chart shows, the Ford 6R80 has a wide gear spread with a low First gear and overdrive in Fifth and Sixth.

1	2	3	4	5	6	R
4.17:1	2.34:1	1.52:1	1.14:1	0.86:1	0.69:1	3.40:1

The 6R80 is a full electronically controlled transmission so everything it does is orchestrated by the car's computer system. The advantage to such a design is a more efficient, longer lasting transmission. While that is what we wanted for the rigors of the road tour, what we needed for the car was a stand-alone control system that told the transmission what to do and when to do it. Fortunately we knew who to call—the crew at Powertrain Control Solutions (PCS).

PCS came into being in 2003 and is under the leadership of Russ Turner and Dan Boucher. A company with a firm foundation made of engineering expertise, not advertising hype, PCS builds products in the United States for OEM, commercial, and the military applications. Problem solving and product development are processes they are extremely familiar with and fortunately for us they've elected to apply their expertise to street rodding as well.

While the Ford 6R80 was a trip into uncharted territory for PCS they had an extensive background in building transmission control modules. Basically the TCM takes in information from senders, such as the TPS and VSS, then tells the transmission when to shift, how hard to shift, and when to lock the converter. In addition the ECM will show OEM diagnostic codes if the transmission malfunctions and provides a "limp" mode to prevent further damage or leaving you parked on the road with a busted gearbox.

ECMS FOR AUTOMATICS

Automatic transmissions have been with us for a long, long time; in fact the basics can be found in the Model T Ford.

At the heart of an automatic transmission are the planetary gear sets. As gears go, planetaries could be considered the most sophisticated. Made up of three elements—a sun gear, ring gear, and planet pinion gears—planetary gear assemblies can provide forward or reverse rotation, a speed increase, constant speed, or a speed reduction (to provide a variety of gear ratios multiple gear sets are used).

In operation, a planetary gear set requires an input (power from the engine), an output (power going out), and a reactor (one of the elements that is held stationary). The gear ratio and the direction of travel depend on which element is performing each function; when none of the elements are held the transmission is in neutral. To keep the reactors stationary bands are used to hold the ring gear to the transmission case, clutch plates and one-way roller clutches are used to hold the planetary elements. In the Tin Lizzie bands were applied mechanically when the driver stepped on a pedal—modern automatic transmissions use hydraulic pressure.

The valvebody is the "brain" of the transmission; it controls shifting by controlling which reactor is applied to what gear set and when. Historically automatic transmissions used hydraulic pressure from a governor, throttle valve, or vacuum modulator to determine shift points but today they use computer-controlled electromechanical servos.

While computer controls have improved the performance and efficiency of modern automatic transmissions, without a Transmission Control Unit (TCU) they're a big, dumb aluminum container of full parts. That means that stuffing one under the floorboards of your custom classic truck has some challenges. But for every problem there is a solution and in this case it comes from the appropriately named Powertrain Control Solutions.

As the experts at PCS explain it, "The primary factor separating the modern electronic automatic transmission from yesterday's hydro-mechanical automatic transmission is the speed and complexity of the logic used for transmission behavior. The hydro-mechanical automatic transmission of yesterday could only make its decisions based on throttle position, engine load, and driveshaft speed. Whereas the TCU can use these inputs as well as torque converter speed, engine speed, wheel speeds, traction control parameters, electronic throttle position, fluid temperature, engine temperature, brake pedal actuation, forward and lateral acceleration, as well as several other parameters. The TCU can also utilize manual shifting operation and provide altered transmission behavior for special conditions (road race, drag race, dynamometer, snow, towing, and so on)."

SIMPLE SHIFT FROM PCS

For those looking for an easy-to-install, effective transmission controller, PCS offers the Simple Shift. No laptops or expensive sessions with a technician are required to completely control shift points, shift firmness, and torque converter lockup. Transmission shift points are adjusted by dials on the end of the control unit and diagnostic capabilities are communicated by flashing LEDs that also indicate what gear the transmission is in and whether or not the torque converter is locked. For those looking for more tuning capabilities the Simple Shift Tuner is also available. The handheld tuner can remain connected to the Simple Shift or be removed when programming is complete.

Installation of the Simple Shift is uncomplicated: mount the unit, hook up the wires, and you're ready to go. The output from the TCU plugs into the factory socket on the transmission, the remaining wires are for signals to the TCU—some are not used while others are, depending on the application.

Output Shaft Speed Sensor (also called the VSS or Vehicle Speed Sensor): For transmission with an Output Shaft Speed Sensor PCS has added a "Y" to the wiring harness, which allows the Simple Shift harness to plug directly into the transmission and still leave an access plug for aftermarket speedometers or factory connectors of some kind that need a VSS signal.

Input Shaft Speed Sensor: If the transmission is equipped, this connector is required for operation.

Throttle Position Sensor: For cable driven–type throttle bodies it's simply a matter of splicing into the existing throttle position sensor wiring. Proper wiring techniques can be found on the support page at powertraincontrolsolutions.com. For carbureted applications a Remote Mount TPS Adapter Kit is included in the Simple Shift Carb kit or available from PCS, PN TCM-6000.

Brake Lamp Input: This is required to unlock the torque converter when the brakes are applied.

Speedometer: This wire is not required for operation of the Simple Shift unit. Its purpose is to deliver a signal to early, older versions of electronic speedometers. Most aftermarket speedometers will use the Output Shaft Speed Signal.

Tachometer: Not required for operation of the Simple Shift unit but it is recommended to offer comprehensive diagnostic capabilities. To utilize the full diagnostic function of your Simple Shift, connect this wire to the tachometer output wire of your ignition system. The tachometer ground wire must also be connected.

PCS Expansion: Not required for operation of the Simple Shift unit, it allows optional equipment, such as the Paddle Shifter or the D200 Touch-Screen Dash logger, to be connected to the Simple Shift system. Instructions on how to utilize this connector will be included in the instructions for the optional expansion kits.

+12V Battery: Required for operation of the Simple Shift unit, it must be connected to the positive terminal of the vehicle's battery. Improper wiring will cause the unit to lose its TPS calibration and will not store diagnostic codes.

Switched +12V: Required for operation it is connected to the ignition/start system of your vehicle. It must have +12 V while in both the start and run positions and no power while in the off position.

Chassis Ground: This wire is required; it is connected to the vehicle's chassis. During the initial installation and before driving the vehicle, the Simple Shift knobs must be set to a baseline configuration described in the instructions and then further adjustments can be made.

Full Throttle Shift Points: PCS recommends this must be done under a controlled environment such as a dragstrip or a chassis dyno so no speed limits are exceeded. Shifts are going to occur at approximately the same rpm for each shift; therefore you may only need to make adjustments using the First to Second shift as a test. To lower the shift point, turn the knob counterclockwise toward the negative numbers. To raise the shift point the knob is turned clockwise toward the positive numbers.

Full Throttle Shift Firmness: If the full throttle shift firmness needs to be decreased, rotate the knob counterclockwise. If the full throttle shifts need to be firmed up, increase the shift firmness by rotating the knob clockwise. When making adjustments, turn the knob by one position then retest. Repeat as necessary. Keep in mind that a softer shift may result in higher engine rpm during the shift, therefore you may have to adjust your high throttle shift point selected in the previous step.

Low/Light Throttle Shift Points: Drive the vehicle at light throttle and adjust the low throttle shift points as necessary. Rotate the knob clockwise to make the shifts occur at a higher rpm. Rotate the knobs counterclockwise to make the shifts happen at a lower rpm.

TCM-2000: Another TCU offered by PCS is the TCM-

2000. Similar to the Simple Shift, the TCM-2000 features dual calibrations that allow the driver to pick from two distinctly different transmission operating modes (sport mode, tow-haul mode, and so on), with programmable shift points, shift firmness, and torque converter lockup tailored to each application. Unique to TCM-2000, PWM outputs are programmable, supporting a wide range of transmissions from GM, Ford, Chrysler, Nissan, Toyota, and others. The CAN interface allows seamless integration with CAN-based vehicles or ECUs and also simplifies the connection to a PCS Paddle Shifter or GSM-2100 Gear Select Module. Installation of the TCM-2000 is similar to the Simple Shift, the TCU is mounted and the wiring harnesses are connected. Next a PC is used to start the TCU software; it will auto-detect the presence of the transmission controller and the current operating parameters of the TCU will appear on the screen. At that point the transmission's functions can be tailored to its intended use. Detailed instructions on tuning the TCU will be found in the user's manual.

REAR AXLE AND DRIVESHAFT

For reasons that are obvious, the Fatman chassis under our AMSOIL/*STREET RODDER* '51 Ford is equipped with a 9-inch Ford rear axle. At the risk of repeating what everyone already knows, these rearends are tough, available with a wide range of gear ratios, and are easy to narrow for custom applications. They've been around forever, and they're still the choice of most street rodders.

Connecting our six-speed automatic to the Fatman 9-inch is a driveshaft from Dynotech. Driveshafts are one of those components that aren't often thought about unless there is a problem—and a bad driveshaft can cause a host of them, including vibration, rapid U-joint wear, and even complete failure of the U-joints or the shaft itself.

Dynotech has a long history in the business of building drivehafts. Formally known as Balance Engineering by General Motors, the company was established in 1923. Today both Balance Engineering and Dynotech are divisions of parent company Micropoise, a manufacturer of tire and wheel balance equipment.

Dynotech's stated mission is to create the best quality and precisely balanced driveshafts for a variety of applications in the automotive industry, while also providing leading diagnostic, corrective, and balancing services. All Dynotech driveshafts are manufactured to order, each offering the company's guaranteed vibration-free warranty. They continue to assemble all of its driveshafts by hand while using modern technologies such as computer welding and high-speed balancing. As a result Dynotech's driveshafts are held to remarkably close

tolerances: U-joint clearances are held to less than 0.002-inch and shaft runout is held to less than 0.010-inch. All driveshafts are balanced to less than 0.20 oz/in, built to within 1/16 inch (0.0625-inch) in length, and are high-speed balanced between 5,000 and 8,000 rpm.

DRIVESHAFT MATERIALS

Dynotech offers driveshafts in steel, aluminum, composite, and hybrid materials.

Steel: Made from DOM (drawn over mandrel) seamless chromoly tubing, these driveshafts are for high-performance street and racing applications. They have higher torque and rpm ratings than OEM shafts and come in 2-, 2-1/2-, 3-, 3-1/2, and 4-inch diameters with 0.065-, 0.083-, and 0.95-wall thickness. Chromoly shafts are for serious racing applications, with increased torsional strength designed to resist well over 2,000 hp. But while they are super strong, a chromoly shaft is significantly heavier than an aluminum shaft of the same size.

Aluminum: These 6061-T6 aluminum shafts are for performance, street, racing, and stock replacement applications. They are lightweight and come in 3-, 3-1/2-, and 4-inch diameters with 0.125-inch wall thickness. Yokes accommodate 1310, 1330, and 1350 series U-joints. Dynotech's aluminum driveshafts can comfortably take up to 1,000 hp and around 900 lb-ft of torque. For 99 percent of performance and race cars out there, the weight savings and high horsepower rating of an aluminum driveshaft would be enough.

Carbon Fiber: Intended for extreme high-performance and racing applications, these shafts are strong, resistant to flex, and they are expensive. They are available in 3-1/2- and 4-inch diameters with steel or aluminum yokes for series 1310, 1330, 1350, and 1410 U-joints

Hybrid: Carbon-fiber–wrapped aluminum driveshafts are for high-performance racing applications. These shafts carry the highest rpm rating and come in 2-3/4-, 3-, and 3-1/2-inch diameters with 0.125-inch wall thickness. Yokes for 1330 and 1350 U-joints are available.

COMMON U-JOINT SIZES

Common U-joint sizes			
Series	1310	1330	1350
Cross length	3-7/32 inch	3-5/8 inch	3-5/8 inch
Cap diameter	1-1/16 inch	1-1/16 inch	1-3/16 inch

ORDERING A DYNOTECH DRIVESHAFT

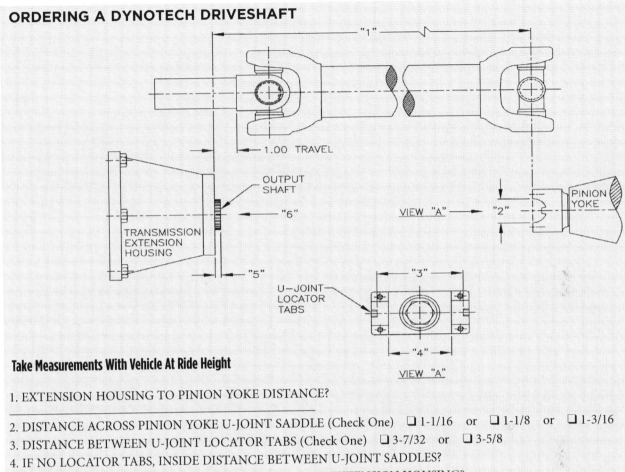

Take Measurements With Vehicle At Ride Height

1. EXTENSION HOUSING TO PINION YOKE DISTANCE?
_____

2. DISTANCE ACROSS PINION YOKE U-JOINT SADDLE (Check One) ❑ 1-1/16 or ❑ 1-1/8 or ❑ 1-3/16

3. DISTANCE BETWEEN U-JOINT LOCATOR TABS (Check One) ❑ 3-7/32 or ❑ 3-5/8

4. IF NO LOCATOR TABS, INSIDE DISTANCE BETWEEN U-JOINT SADDLES?

5. DISTANCE BETWEEN END OF OUTPUT SHAFT AND EXTENSION HOUSING?

6. DOES THE OUTPUT SHAFT HAVE A THREADED HOLE IN THE END?   ❑ YES   ❑ NO

7. COUNT THE NUMBER OF SPLINES ON THE TRANS OUTPUT SHAFT.

8. CHECK THE SHAFT MATERIAL YOU WISH TO PURCHASE.

❑ DOM Steel (Stock & Racing)

❑ Seam Tube Steel (OEM Replacement)

❑ 6061-T6 Aluminum (Street Rod)

❑ Other_____ Diameter: _____

9. WHAT TYPE OF TRANSMISSION ARE YOU USING?
_____

10. NAME _____
ADDRESS _____
CITY_____ STATE_____ ZIP_____ PHONE NUMBER
EMAIL _____

IF YOU HAVE ANY QUESTIONS PLEASE CALL (800) 633-5559

1731 Thorncroft
Troy, Michigan 48084-5302
Telephone (248) 362-2777
Fax (248) 362-3886
dynotechengineering.com

❯ The 3.5 EcoBoost block is "open deck" with steel sleeves molded in. Heads have high efficiency four-valve pent roof combustion chambers with 1.456-intake and 1.220-inch exhaust valves.

❯ Both exhaust manifolds have small 1.18-inch outlets that connect to the turbos; the exhaust pipes coming out of the turbos are 2-1/2 inches in diameter.

❯ Part of the secret to the EcoBoost's outstanding performance is this Garrett watercooled turbocharger on the right side.

❯ With one of the covers removed, the twin camshaft arrangement can be seen. For our application the variable cam timing sprockets were locked out with components from COMP Cams.

❯ The other part of the secret is the mirror image turbo on the left side of the engine. By using two small turbos the lag usually associated with these superchargers is virtually eliminated.

❯ George Klass, of Accufab, supplied a cable-operated throttle body from a 4.6L modular motor to replace the original drive-by-wire unit. The clamshell clamp and piping are also courtesy of Accufab (accufabracing.com).

❯ A test-fit of the engine and transmission made it clear that firewall/toeboard/ trans tunnel modifications were in order.

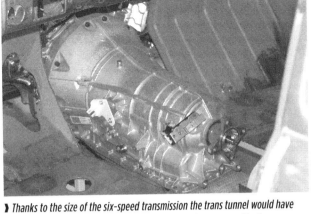

❯ Thanks to the size of the six-speed transmission the trans tunnel would have to be quite large. Note the flange on the output shaft as opposed to the more common splined configuration.

❯ The firewall was opened up using a Miller Electric Mfg. Co. plasma cutter.

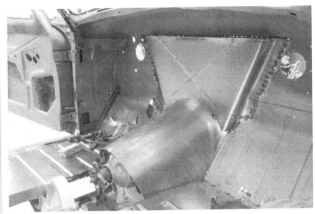

❯ After the test-fit, the Honest Charley Garage team fabricated a new firewall section and transmission tunnel.

❯ After positioning the engine and transmission, the amount of protrusion into the passenger compartment could be determined.

❯ By rolling the edges of the insert and adding stiffening beads the recess in the firewall looks as though it could have come from the factory.

❱ Simple steel motor mount brackets were fabricated from steel plate; the rubber cushions are early Ford ('32-48 style).

❱ Plastic pipe was used by the Honest Charley Garage crew to mock up the turbo inlet and intercooler plumbing.

❱ Turbochargers compress air and that creates heat. To keep the temperature of the engine's air supply under control is an air-to-air intercooler.

❱ The finished stainless plumbing is a definite improvement over the plastic.

❱ The intercooler mounts in front of the radiator and A/C condenser and has the inlet and outlet on the passenger side.

❱ Twin turbos certainly complicate the intercooler plumbing, but the performance gains are worth the effort.

❯ Things are crowded on the left side of the engine but there was plenty of room to connect onto the Flaming River rack-and-pinion. Note the exhaust pipe from the turbocharger has been wrapped with insulation.

❯ The FAST XFI controller for the fuel injection and the XIM ignition module were mounted on the inside of the firewall adjacent to the Vintage Air underdash unit.

❯ FAST supplied the Extreme ignition ECU along with a Coyote V-8 wiring harness with two coil leads removed. Controlling the fuel injection is an XFI 2.0 ECU.

❯ The FAST XFI controller uses wideband oxygen sensors to determine the air/fuel ratio and make the necessary adjustments.

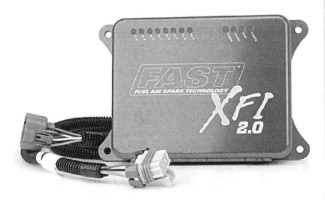

❯ FAST's XFI controller learns how to adjust the air/fuel ratios to meet the targets established during setup. It's like having a tune-up expert on board at all times.

❯ A coolant temperature sensor, or CTS, is the "choke" in an EFI system.

❱ This is a FAST air temperature sensor (ATS).

❱ For the ultimate in flexibility, PCS offers the TCM-2000. This user-friendly ECU provides complete control over an electronic transmission's operation in two separate modes, such as street and sport.

❱ The throttle position sensor mounts directly to the throttle body. It's used by the EFI controller, as well as the transmission's computer in automatic applications.

❱ The Simple Shift from PCS is the perfect solution for those who want an overdrive electronic transmission in their car without a complicated control system. Set the knobs that control the shift points, shift firmness, when the converter locks and unlocks, as well as the number of cylinders the engine has when you're done—it's that simple.

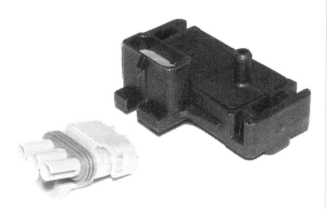

❱ As this engine is supercharged, FAST provided a two-bar MAP sensor that can read full vacuum and up to 15 pounds of boost.

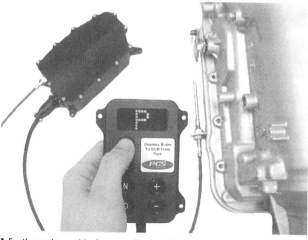

❱ For those who want to do away with the shift lever, PCS offers the GSM push-button shifter. A proven device, its been thoroughly tested in automotive, military, commercial, and agricultural applications.

❯ The PCS Paddle Shifter puts upshift and downshift at the driver's fingertips. The unique paddle shifter is powered by simply attaching to the horn button wire, eliminating any external wiring on the column.

❯ All Dynotech driveshafts are checked for straightness and balanced. Dynotech TIG welds all balancing weights to ensure that they never come off.

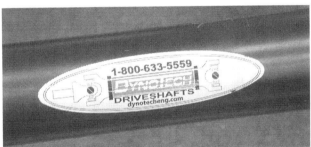

❯ With a new Dynotech driveshaft just a phone call away, cutting and modifying an old driveshaft isn't worth the time and annoyance of living with less than stellar results.

❯ We pointed out the flange on the output shaft of the transmission; as a result the slip joint is built into the driveshaft.

❯ Dynotech driveshafts are available with steel, aluminum, carbon-fiber, or hybrid tubes. They can build and ship most custom driveshafts in 72 hours or less.

Four-Wheel Discs

✳ BY RON CERIDONO ✳ PHOTOGRAPHY BY THE AUTHOR ✳

❯ The 2013 AMSOIL/STREET RODDER Road Tour Ford rides on a Fatman Fabrications chassis with QA1 coilovers and Wilwood disc brakes at all four corners.

When the new Fords were introduced there were many exterior changes and even more that couldn't be seen. The entirely new chassis was hidden from view, but improvements in ride, handling, and stopping were all obvious to anyone familiar with Ford's pre-'49 offerings.

Ford was the last major manufacturer to convert from mechanical brakes to hydraulic. That change took place in 1939 and with the exception of a change in the brake shoes' anchors the basic design remained the same through 1948.

In 1949 Fords were equipped with larger Bendix-style brakes—the early hydraulic brakes featured 162 square inches of lining area with 12x1.75 shoes compared to 177 square inches with 10x2.25 shoes for 1949. But the real advantage to the new brakes was in the basic design. Ford's original hydraulics had the bottom of each brake shoe securely anchored independently to the backing plate. With the Bendix design the brake shoes are hooked together at the bottom and attached to the backing plates in such a manner that they can move slightly. During braking, the front, or primary, brake shoe makes contact with the drum and tries to rotate with it. The movement of the front shoe forces the rear, or secondary shoe, into the drum with increased force. This design is referred to as "self-energizing" and it provides a noticeable increase in stopping power.

Brakes work on a simple principle: Friction between a stationary and a moving surface, but friction creates heat and heat is the enemy of brakes. As the braking surfaces become hotter the coefficient of friction between them is reduced and effectiveness is lost. The term that is often used to describe this is brake fade. If you've

❯ *The Forged Billet Dynalite caliper is a four-piston and used in many of Wilwood's bolt-on disc brake kits. Mounted to the aluminum hubs are cross-drilled, slotted, and ventilated 11-inch rotors.*

ever driven a car down a steep grade and found it took more and more brake pedal pressure to slow the car, you've experienced brake fade.

The ability to dissipate heat has a great deal to do with the effectiveness of brakes and this is where discs have a huge advantage over drums. As the caliper only covers a small part of a disc brake's friction surface, a large portion of the rotor is exposed to air, which keeps it relatively cool. With a drum brake most of the friction surface is in contact with the brake shoes, which leaves little surface area for cooling. Consequently, compared

to discs, drum brakes get hotter faster and stay hot longer. During hard or continuous use that reduces their efficiency noticeably.

Another factor that allows disc brakes to function more effectively than drums is the wiping action inherent in their design. In wet conditions the brake pads tend to wipe water off the rotor. With drums, moisture can become trapped between the shoes and drum, which lowers the coefficient of friction considerably until the water is dispersed.

CALIPERS

Basically, there are three types of calipers: fixed, sliding, and floating. Fixed calipers are mounted solidly to a mounting bracket with one, two, or more pistons per side to apply the pads. When multiple pistons are used on each side they are more or less in a row, consequently the caliper can utilize a longer pad more effectively than a single-piston caliper. The combination of multiple pistons and large friction surfaces mean that fixed calipers can supply a tremendous amount of stopping power.

While fixed calipers are very

effective, they are more complicated to manufacture. Since there are pistons on both sides of the caliper, fluid must be delivered to both sides of the caliper. That means small external lines or well-sealed interior passages must be provided to connect the two halves.

Another caliper design is the sliding style. These have a single piston on just one side and work like a C-clamp. The piston pushes the inside brake pad against the rotor, once it makes contact, the caliper slides in its bracket and pulls the outside pad against the rotor. Ford and Chrysler used this style brake.

Similar to the sliding caliper is the floating design (typically single-piston GM calipers). Like the sliding caliper, floating calipers apply hydraulic pressure to one pad, then the caliper, which "floats" on a pair of mounting pins, pulls the other pad against the rotor. While the sliding and floating calipers work in a similar fashion, there is one major difference. With the sliding style, the braking force is transferred to the caliper, which means it must be a stout piece. With a floating caliper, the mounting bracket captures the pads. As a result the caliper doesn't have to be as beefy.

TYPES OF DISCS

Although disc brake rotors come in a wide variety of shapes and sizes, they can be broken down into just two categories, solid and vented. Solid rotors are just that, a simple, flat rotor. Simple and inexpensive, the disadvantage to solid rotors is their limited ability to get rid of heat when compared to the vented style. While solid rotors are adequate for lightweight cars, particularly on the rear, a better disc brake rotor option for heavier vehicles is the ventilated style. This design separates the two friction surfaces with air passages to aid in cooling.

MASTER CYLINDERS

At the heart of the brake system is the master cylinder. It transfers the mechanical force applied to the pedal to the hydraulic fluid.

There are two types of master cylinders: single reservoir, single outlet master cylinders like those that were original on '49-51 Fords; and dual reservoir, dual outlet (tandem) master cylinders. A single fluid output master cylinder will be plumbed to all four wheels while a tandem master cylinder will have two fluid output ports, one for the front brakes and one for the rear.

When selecting a master cylinder the goal is to pick one that supplies sufficient fluid volume to provide a firm, responsive pedal, while generating enough pressure to stop the car comfortably. The master cylinder bore size is dependent on several variables. Choosing a master cylinder bore size begins with defining how the master cylinder will be actuated, manually or with the assistance

of a booster, either hydraulic or vacuum operated. The combined piston area and piston volume of your calipers and the pedal ratio are also major considerations. Remember that a larger master cylinder bore produces more volume and a smaller master cylinder bore produces more pressure. The best way determine the appropriate master cylinder bore for your specific application is to review Wildwood's Tech Tip Guide. You can also contact a Wilwood Sales Technician at (805) 388-1188, or email customerreply@wilwood.com.

PEDAL RATIOS

Pedal ratio, or mechanical leverage, is the ratio calculated from the length from the pivot point of the pedal to the center of the foot pedal divided by the length from the pivot point to the master cylinder pushrod.

With a 1-inch master cylinder, 100 pounds pushing on the pedal, and the pedal having a 4:1 ratio, the force is 4 x 100 = 400 pounds. With a 100-pound push on the pedal, and the pedal having a 6:1 ratio, the force is 6 x 100 = 600 pounds.

If you're uncertain about which pedal ratio is right for your application, a 6:1 ratio is an excellent starting point.

BOOSTERS

Power brakes are something that most of us expect to find on new cars, and they're common on street rods as well. However they aren't as necessary as most builders seem to think they are, and with a properly sized master cylinder, they're simply not required.

While our Road Tour car is not equipped with a booster here is an overview of the types commonly used:

Vacuum

The most common type of brake booster is the vacuum style. A fairly simple device, they are basically a canister divided into two chambers by a diaphragm. On one side of the diaphragm are the brake pedal and a vent to atmospheric pressure; on the other side is a pushrod to the master cylinder and a hose leading to the intake manifold—vacuum draws the air out of the master cylinder side of the booster, while atmospheric pressure is present on the brake pedal side. The higher pressure on the brake pedal side simply helps apply more mechanical pressure to the master cylinder.

Hydraulic

This type of booster taps into the power steering line and uses hydraulic pressure to supplement the pedal pressure applied to the master cylinder.

Hydraulic boosters are often found on diesel engines as the vacuum type won't work (diesels don't have manifold vacuum), but they work on gas engines just as well. (GM used them on a variety of diesel cars and trucks and Ford/Mercury used them in the '70s on some of their larger, gas-powered cars.) While hydraulic boosters are ideal for diesels, they also work well on gas that have low manifold vacuum as the result of an aggressive camshaft.

In operation fluid flows from the power steering pump through the brake booster and then onto the steering box. The steering box and the brake booster both have return lines, and to accommodate them the pumps used in these applications normally have two return fittings.

When the brakes aren't in use, fluid flows through the booster to the steering box. But when the brake pedal is depressed, pressurized fluid flows through a spool valve into a chamber in the booster. There the fluid applies pressure to a piston, which pushes on the master cylinder providing the power assist.

Also part of the system is a device called an accumulator (some are on the unit, others are remote) that stores enough pressurized fluid for at least one assisted application of the brakes if the engine quits. After that the brakes behave as though there was no assist.

Electric Boosters

Something new on the brake booster scene is the electric type. Used in conjunction with a special master cylinder, hydraulic pressure in the area of 2,500 psi is created by an electric pump. That pressure is then delivered to a special master cylinder used in these systems.

BRAKE LINES AND VALVES

One of the common misconceptions about brake plumbing is that there is a relationship between brake line size and hydraulic pressure—there isn't. The master cylinder establishes the pressure in a brake system; all the lines do is deliver the pressurized fluid. Brake lines are most often 3/16- or 1/4-inch diameter and, while there will be no pressure difference between the two, there will be a difference in the amount of fluid delivered. The bigger tubing will carry more volume, so 1/4-inch line may be preferable in some instances (disc brake calipers with large piston displacements).

Regardless of the size, when it comes to selecting the type of rigid brake lines to use, there are only two choices: steel or stainless steel. Copper or aluminum should never be used and excessively long lengths of flex line, including the braided variety, should not be used, as a spongy pedal will result. When plumbing a chassis, brake and fuel lines should be a minimum of 3 inches away from any significant heat sources, most notably the exhaust system.

A variety of valves may be found in a modern brake system:

Metering

Metering valves, also called hold-off valve, are used in the brake system to better balance the front to rear brakes. The valve does not allow the pressure to rise at the front disc brakes until the pressure at the rear drums has risen sufficiently to overcome the brake shoe springs. At this point the valve opens to allow full pressure to build at the front brakes.

Proportioning

Proportioning valves modulate the pressure in the hydraulic system. They are commonly used to minimize rear wheel lockup found in heavy braking and compensate for differences in braking conditions in front disc/rear drum systems. Wilwood's adjustable proportioning allows pressure adjustments range from 100-1,000 psi and provide for a maximum decrease of 57 percent inline pressure. This adjustment lets you fine-tune the front to rear braking balance by proportionally decreasing the rear (or in some cases the front) brake line pressure.

Residual

Residual valves maintain a small amount of pressure in drum brake systems to keep the wheel cylinder cups expanded. This prevents air from being drawn into the system and allows the brakes to react quicker. A 10-pound valve is common in drum brake systems.

Normally disc brake systems don't have residual pressure valves, however, when the master cylinder is mounted below the floor, and is lower than the calipers, a 2-pound valve may be necessary to prevent the calipers from draining fluid back to the master cylinder.

Combination Valves

A combination valve incorporates metering and proportioning functions into one valve. These are available for disc/drum or drum/drum systems and often have warning light provisions to indicate if one half of a dual brake system has lost pressure.

BRINGING THE ROAD TOUR CAR TO A STOP

Although the original brakes on the AMSOIL/*STREET RODDER* Road Tour '51 Ford were state of the art then, they're relics by today's standards. To meet the demands to today's driving environment we stepped up to four-wheel disc brakes from the best-known names in aftermarket brakes, Wilwood. Since it was founded in 1977 the company has designed and manufactured brakes for all types of competitive motorsports, agricultural equipment, industrial applications, utility vehicles, snowmobiles, quads, motorcycles, military vehicles, and of course, street rods. They stock over 300 different brake calipers, 200 rotor designs, 100 master cylinder designs, and a wide assortment of brackets, fittings, valves, and brake lines. Off-the-shelf brake calipers range in size from tiny calipers used on go-karts and light-duty industrial equipment to heavy-duty original equipment brakes for the U.S. military Humvee. In short, if you've got something that needs brakes, Wilwood has the parts to make it happen.

Up front the Honest Charley Garage crew equipped the Road Tour Ford with Wilwood's FDL Pro-Series Front Hub Kit with forged billet Dynalite calipers. This kit provides state-of-the-art braking into a package compact enough to fit inside popular 15-inch wheels. FDL Pro-Series kits can be used with either manual or power boost master cylinders. In the rear a Dynapro Low-Profile Pro-Series rear disc brake kit was used. It includes forged billet Dynapro Low-Profile four-piston calipers 11.00-inch one-piece hat and rotor assemblies, and high friction pads. The neatly hidden internal shoe system provides a clean installation with superior static holding power for parking. Optional caliper finishes and rotor designs enable the builder to personalize the style and optimize brake performance for every individual application.

Supplying the hydraulic pressure for our four-wheel disc brakes is a Wilwood 260-9439-BK tandem chamber master cylinder. Fully machined from a high-pressure die casting of a premium alloy, these master cylinders incorporate a slotted mounting flange to accommodate bolt centers between 3.22 to 3.40 inches and also features side-hole mounts on 6.40-inch centers. These master cylinders have a full separation between the front and rear chambers and dual outlets allow for right- or left-hand plumbing based on mount location. Wilwood's Tandem Aluminum Master Cylinder is available in 3 bore sizes, 7/8, 1, and 1.125 inches; and three finishes, plain, ball burnished, and black e-coat. They're designed to fit most mounting flanges, and feature outlet ports on both sides for multiple plumbing options.

To provide a means of adjusting brake balance a Wilwood 260-11179 proportioning valve was plumbed into the system. This redesigned valve substantially simplifies mounting, plumbing, wiring, and brake proportioning adjustments on vehicles with custom brake systems. The combination block maintains full isolation between front and rear fluid circuits and can be used in conjunction with any tandem outlet or dual mount master cylinder assemblies. The rear circuit has a single inlet and single outlet with the adjustable proportioning valve. The front circuit has a single inlet with two outlets. It can be run as a single outlet with one outlet plugged, or used to split the plumbing on its way to the front calipers. Also installed in the system were 260-1874 RPV, 2-pound inline residual pressure valves. These retain a minimum brake line pressure to help eliminate excessive pedal travel in both disc and

drum brake systems. When used in disc brake applications where the master cylinder is mounted below the horizontal plane of the calipers and fluid drain back occurs from gravity and vibration, thereby causing excessive caliper piston retraction and a longer brake pedal stroke. The minimal 2-pound residual pressure prevents fluid from flowing back without causing the brakes to drag.

WILWOOD FAQS

With Wilwood's array of offerings they can supply almost any brake component required and answer just about any question on the subject. Here are some of the most frequently asked questions and their replies:

Q: I have a soft pedal. How do I cure the problem?

A: Assuming that your spongy pedal is related to the brake installation and not aggressive braking, such as that experienced during racing, the most likely culprit is air in the system. See above for proper bleeding of the master cylinder and brake system. A spongy pedal can also occur for a number of other reasons: misaligned caliper, incorrect caliper/master cylinder bore combination, and more. See Wilwood's complete Troubleshooting Guide for a more thorough list of causes and solutions. You can also contact a Wilwood Sales Technician at (805) 388-1188 or email customerreply@wilwood.com.

Q: I have a hard pedal, but the car is very difficult to stop. What is the problem?

A: Common contributors to "hard pedal, won't stop" issues are an oversized master cylinder bore and/or inadequate pedal lever ratio. Another contributing factor is the "aggressiveness" of the pad. Disc brakes require approximately 900-1,200 psi at the caliper for effective functioning. We recommend that you use Wilwood Quick Check Pressure Gauges to measure your pressure at the caliper. If you are not generating the required pressure, we recommend increasing your pedal ratio, or going to a smaller bore master cylinder. See Wilwood's Troubleshooting Guide for more complete information, and make sure you have Wilwood Quick Check Pressure Gauges available to assist you in evaluating the problem.

Q: Why does my pedal "fade" or "go away" after I've warmed up my brakes?

A: Old brake fluid is the main cause of this problem. Brake fluid deterioration occurs from heat cycling and absorption of moisture. As brake temperatures increase, the old fluid boils, causing the pedal to fade. See Wilwood's "lose your pedal" section of the Troubleshooting Guide, and make sure you are using fresh Wilwood brake fluid.

Q: When are residual pressure valves required?

A: These inline pressure valves retain a minimum brake line pressure to help eliminate excessive pedal travel in both disc and drum brake systems. The 2-pound valve is used in disc brake applications where the master cylinder is mounted below the horizontal plane of the calipers and fluid drain back occurs from gravity and vibration, thereby causing excessive caliper piston retraction and a longer brake pedal stroke. The minimal 2-pound residual pressure prevents fluid from flowing back without causing the brakes to drag. With drum brakes, a 10-pound valve is used to compensate for return spring tension in the drums.

Q: What is a proportioning valve and do I need one?

A: A proportioning valve is a pressure reduction device. It is typically installed in the rear brake line to reduce braking efficiency and compensate for premature rear-wheel lockup; a result of incorrect front to rear brake bias. An adjustable proportioning valve permits incremental adjustments to fine-tune brake bias. This ability to adjust front-rear brake bias is particularly important in race applications, as changing track conditions and vehicle dynamics usually require the brake bias be adjusted throughout the race.

Normally, you do not need to purchase a proportioning valve with a Wilwood four-wheel disc brake kit. Because Wilwood manufactures calipers with the correct piston area for each application, Wilwood kits will work with your dual-chamber stock master cylinder and stock pressure limiting valve. However, if you significantly change your vehicle's weight and/or chassis dynamics, such as is common with muscle cars, hot rods, street machines, and customs, you will likely need to remove the factory proportioning valve and install an adjustable proportioning valve when installing Wilwood brake kits. The factory valve was designed for a specific weight car, on a specific tire, with a specific suspension system, and a specific amount of brake torque at each wheel. If any of these specifications have been altered, the factory valve will not allow optimum performance of the braking system by either limiting too much pressure, or not limiting the pressure adequately. A Wilwood adjustable proportioning valve will provide easy adjustment to obtain the optimum pressure for your modified vehicle.

Q: What brake fluid should I use?

A: The Department of Transportation specifies three common types of brake fluid: DOT 3, DOT 4, and DOT 5. DOTs 3 or 4 are the preferred types for high performance, high temperature use, and are available in a very wide range of formulations and performance characteristics. DOT 3 fluids are usually less expensive than DOT 4 fluids and are less capable in extreme use. DOT 5 is a silicon-based fluid that's not good for high temperature use (it expands, becomes compressible, and makes your pedal soft and spongy). DOT 5 is inert and not corrosive, which makes it good for preserving classic cars because it doesn't take your paint off in the event of accidental spillage or leak.

Wilwood has versions of each DOT fluid engineered to the specific needs of our customers. Wilwood Hi-Temp is the maximum performance DOT 3 fluid at cost-effective price. Wilwood EXP DOT 4 fluid is the highest temperature, highest performance, lowest compressibility brake fluid you can buy. Wilwood's DOT 5 fluid is formulated to protect your classic vehicle and give reliable brake performance.

Q: What master cylinder bore size do I need?

A: The master cylinder bore size is dependent on several variables. Choosing a master cylinder bore size begins with defining how the master cylinder will be actuated, manually or with the assistance of a booster, either hydraulic or vacuum operated. Once you have decided on how the master cylinder will be actuated, the information below can be used as a guideline for selecting the right master cylinder. Keep in mind that auto manufacturers have put many years of experience and a lot of testing into determining the right combination for a given car, and when building a custom car with changes to the suspension, brakes, tires, and weight balance, you too may need to do some testing to determine which master cylinder is right for your vehicle.

The combined piston area and piston volume of your calipers and the pedal ratio are two of the primary considerations. Is the system boosted or not is another consideration. Remember that a larger master cylinder bore produces more volume and a smaller master cylinder bore produces more pressure. To determine the appropriate master cylinder bore for your specific application, review Wilwood's Tech Tip Guide.

Q: What master cylinder is best suited for my application?

A: The goal is to select a master cylinder system that supplies sufficient fluid volume to provide a firm, responsive pedal, while generating enough pressure to stop the car comfortably. There are two types of master cylinders, single reservoir, single outlet master cylinders; and dual reservoir, dual outlet (tandem) master cylinders. A tandem master cylinder will have two fluid output ports, one for the front brakes and one for the rear. A single fluid output master cylinder, or "fruit jar", will be plumbed to all four calipers as a single system.

Dual master cylinder pedal systems are used extensively in race cars and have completely separate master cylinder systems for the front and rear brakes. This setup permits easy adjustment of front to rear brake bias with the integrated balance bar assembly.

Q: How do I bench bleed my master cylinder?

A: Place your master cylinder in a vise, holding it by the mounting bracket and making sure it is level. Thread a 38x24-inch threaded barb fitting into each of the pressure ports, then attach a 6-inch piece of clear plastic hose to each barb. Fill the reservoir with new brake fluid and then place the other end of each hose into the reservoir; one on each side of the wall separating the two chambers. The hoses must remain submerged in brake fluid until the bleeding process is completed. Using full strokes, slowly push the piston in using a Phillips head screwdriver or other device that simulates a pushrod. Do this until all the air bubbles have disappeared from the clear plastic hose.

Q: I put your front and rear kits on my vehicle, but the pedal goes to the floor, what is causing this to happen?

A: Other causes include: air in the brake system, calipers not bled with bleed screws straight up, wrong size master cylinder (too small), calipers mounted on an equal plane with or higher than the master cylinder, calipers flex excessively due to excessive pressure (over 1,200 psi), or pedal ratio too great and excessive spindle deflection in corners causing piston knock-back. For further information review Wilwood's Trouble Shooting Guide.

Q: How do I bleed the system when installing brake calipers, lines, and hoses?

A: Always bench bleed the master cylinder first (see above), then the system. Make sure all calipers have bleed screws facing upward to fully evacuate air from the system. Wilwood calipers with internal fluid passages and four bleed screws (two on each end) require only the upward facing bleed screws to be bled. Start bleeding the bleed screw farthest from the master cylinder (typically the right rear caliper outboard half), and work toward the one nearest the master cylinder.

The most common method to bleed a system is to manually pump the pedal. This process is as follows: Pedal bleeding requires two people: one person pumps the pedal, and the other operates the bleed valves. First, connect a plastic hose to the valve on the outboard body bleed screw farthest away from the master cylinder. Submerge the other end of the hose in a container of brake fluid to ensure that no air is siphoned back into the system. Have the person in the vehicle depress the pedal and hold it at the floor. With the pedal on the floor, the person at the caliper should open the bleed screw one-quarter of a turn to allow the accumulated air and fluid to evacuate. Once the air and fluid have stopped flowing out of the bleeder valve, close it. Now, the person in the vehicle should slowly pump the pedal to refill the calipers with fluid. Once a firm pedal has been achieved, the pedal operator should depress the pedal and hold it, repeating the above sequence. Make sure that the reservoir of the master cylinder does not run out of fluid, as this will introduce air into the system. Continue in this manner until all calipers are bled on both the inboard and outboard bleed screw. You may have to repeat the process for optimal results. Three other methods to bleed a system are gravity, pressure, and vacuum.

❯ In the rear are Wilwood's forged billet Dynalite four-piston calipers with high-friction pads. The two-piece hat and rotor assemblies feature internal parking brake mechanisms.

❯ Wilwood's Dynalite calipers utilize four pistons and are available with piston areas of 3.0, 4.12, or 4.80 square inches and can accommodate rotors up to 1.250 inches wide. Finish options are black anodize, black or red powdercoating, and polished.

❯ Another popular caliper from Wilwood is the four-piston Dynapro. Like the Dynalite, it is available in a lug mount configuration.

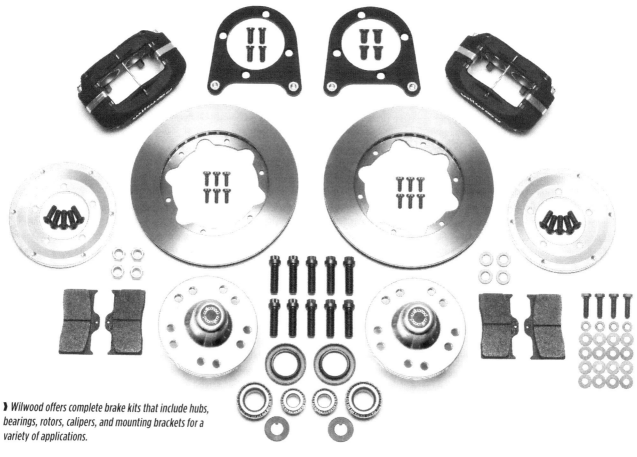

❯ Wilwood offers complete brake kits that include hubs, bearings, rotors, calipers, and mounting brackets for a variety of applications.

❯ This is an exploded view of a typical Wilwood FDL front disc brake kit.

THESE COMPONENTS ARE INCLUDED WITH THE WILWOOD PROSPINDLE KIT

WILWOOD PROSPINDLE KIT, P/N 830-9807 SOLD SEPARATELY

SRP DRILLED/SLOTTED PATTERN ROTOR

LEFT HAND, DRIVERS SIDE SHOWN

❯ Many of the Wilwood kits use rotors that separate from the hubs. Note the hubs are drilled for Chevy and Ford bolt patterns.

❯ A variety of rotors are available with Wilwood's rear disc brake kits (these are ventilated but not drilled and slotted). Note the multiple wheel bolt patterns.

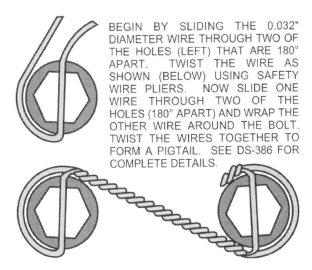

BEGIN BY SLIDING THE 0.032" DIAMETER WIRE THROUGH TWO OF THE HOLES (LEFT) THAT ARE 180° APART. TWIST THE WIRE AS SHOWN (BELOW) USING SAFETY WIRE PLIERS. NOW SLIDE ONE WIRE THROUGH TWO OF THE HOLES (180° APART) AND WRAP THE OTHER WIRE AROUND THE BOLT. TWIST THE WIRES TOGETHER TO FORM A PIGTAIL. SEE DS-386 FOR COMPLETE DETAILS.

❯ This is Wilwood's recommended procedure for installing safety wire in the rotor screws.

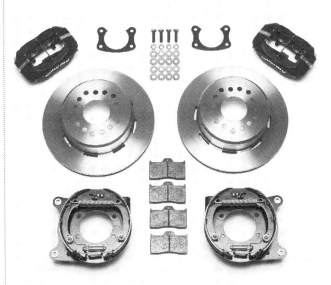

❯ Installing rear disc brakes has been simplified by the introduction of rotors incorporating drums housing internal expanding parking brake assemblies.

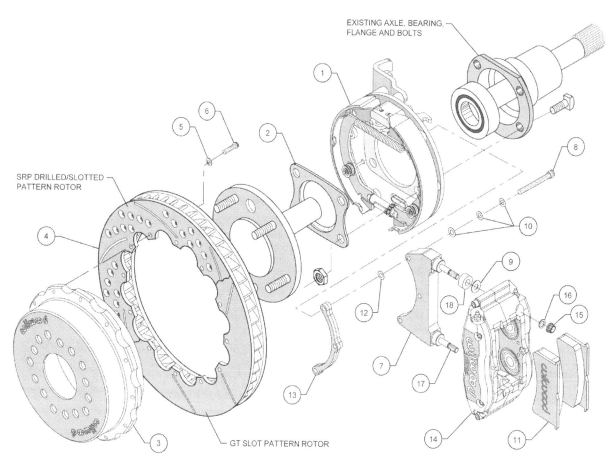

EXISTING AXLE, BEARING, FLANGE AND BOLTS

SRP DRILLED/SLOTTED PATTERN ROTOR

GT SLOT PATTERN ROTOR

❱ This exploded view shows the components of a typical Wilwood rear disc brake kit.

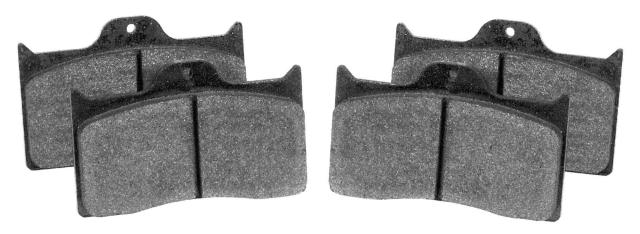

❱ Wilwood brake pads come in a variety of compositions to accommodate applications from street to racetrack.

❱ Brake rotors are available in every conceivable configuration—solid, vented, drilled, slotted, and combinations of them all.

❱ Wilwood's 2-psi residual pressure valves are used to prevent the fluid draining from disc brake calipers when the master cylinder is mounted low on the chassis. Ten-pound valves are available for drum brakes.

❱ To adjust front to rear brake bias Wilwood offers this adjustable proportioning valve.

❱ Wilwood's dual chamber master cylinder offers a variety of mounting options (flange or frame mount) and brake line outlets (left or right side).

Making our Shoebox Ford Whole Again

✳ *BY GERRY BURGER* ✳

✳ *PHOTOGRAPHY BY THE AUTHOR* ✳

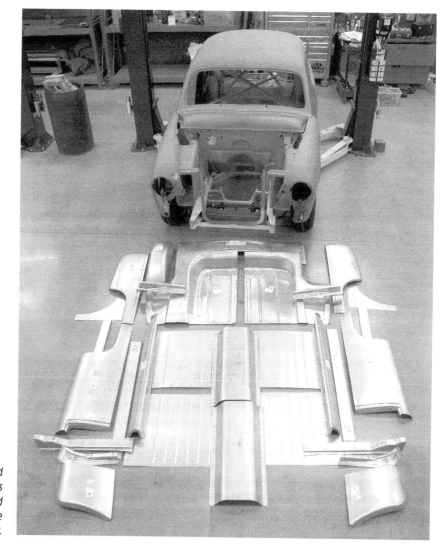

❱ *When the shipment of Dennis Carpenter Ford Restoration Parts (DCFRP) replacement panels arrived at the Honest Charley Garage we spread them out in front of our '51 Ford project car. We used every piece repairing the car.*

Anyone reading this knows full well building a street rod is a tricky deal. Until you have that body down to bare metal you are never certain exactly what you are working on. Flintstone Media Blasting removed all the paint, dirt, grime, and rust from our project '51 Ford and what was uncovered was daunting. Not only did this old Ford have a lot of rust, it even had rusted-out patch panels that had been installed many years ago.

When rust is this extensive you may consider finding a better body, but happily the team at Honest Charley Garage felt this was a good opportunity to show that rough and rusty can be converted into solid steel with time, tools, and talent, along with repair panels from Dennis Carpenter Ford Restoration Parts. The Honest Charley Garage team of Greg Cunningham, Delton Scott, Richard Marter, and Jonathan Myren would be performing the salvage operation on our '51 Ford.

The car had been cross-braced with angle iron and box tubing prior to being sent to the media blaster so no structural twisting or bending would occur. Now it was time to restore the structural integrity to the body. The rust was extensive enough that the cross bracing was the only thing maintaining the body shape.

The first step was to cut out the rusted main floor section to expose the body mounts that attach to the bottom of the floor. Cut-off wheels and the occasional Sawzall removed the rusted metal with ease, exposing the channel body mounts, or at least what was left of them. With the body mounts exposed it became apparent that the first order of business would be repairing the rusty lower cowl area.

❱ Like so many old cars, the '51 Tudor sedan looked much better in weathered black paint; there was a host of surprises lying beneath the aged paint.

❱ The good news is the Ford rides on a brand-new Fatman Fabrications chassis, so there will be no rust repair on the frame.

❱ We knew it wasn't exactly "rust free" but when Flintstone Media finished with the body we could see through most panels.

❱ Delton Scott spent many hours going over the body with a DA sander cleaning up bare metal and removing any small areas not cleaned with the media blasting.

This repair was a matter of fabricating box panels to replace the lower rusted pieces and connecting it to the toeboard portion of the floorboard. These repair panels were formed by Honest Charley Garage and welded in place using a combination of a MIG welding with a Millermatic 211 and TIG welding with a Miller Dynasty 200 machine. Once the lower corner of the cowl was repaired the lower portion of the doorjamb was repaired in preparation for the installation of the new Dennis Carpenter Ford Restoration Parts inner and outer rocker panels.

The inner rocker panel was tack-welded in place on the inside of the rocker panel prior to fitting it to the body. Happily, our door opening was the exact same size as the replacement rocker panel so we felt certain the door opening had not been compromised. A little tweaking on the repaired corners and the Dennis Carpenter Ford Restoration Parts rocker panel was tack welded in place. The door was then installed to be certain the opening was correct and the gaps were all uniform between the new rocker panel and the door. The gaps were nearly perfect and after a

bit of adjustment the gaps were better than any new '51 Ford. The door was removed and the rocker panels were welded in place. We now had the cowl connected to the rest of the body and the inner rocker panels provide the mounting surface for the body mounts.

The body mounts were test-fit alongside the original mounts before cutting out the old rusted units. Delton Scott cut the new Dennis Carpenter Ford Restoration Parts body mount and formed a 3/8-inch flange that fit flush with the new inner rocker panels. The new

❱ Jonathon Myren laid down a protective layer of epoxy primer over the entire body and all the disassembled panels.

❱ Resting in the Honest Charley Garage spray booth the body already looks a lot better, but don't let this picture deceive you. This is one rusty old car.

mounts were bolted to the Fatman Fabrications chassis and then tack welded in place to the inner rocker. During rust repair it is best to tack weld all your panels prior to finish welding. Most of these panels connect to one another so it may be necessary to go back and move one repair panel to line up with the next panel, and tack welding makes such adjustment easy.

Moving to the rear, a similar process secured the second body mount from the rocker panel to the body mount on the frame. Certain that everything was properly located, the mounts, rocker panels, and inner rocker panels received the finished welding in preparation for floor installation.

On our extensively rusted '51 the entire front floor was replaced, once again Dennis Carpenter Ford Restoration Parts repair panels saved the team at Honest Charley Garage a lot of time. The floors were fitted inside the car and tack welded in place. The floors and transmission tunnel are not exact replicas of the original, rather they are designed to be cut and fit to each application.

For that reason we used portions of the front flooring, leaving any good original metal in place. In the area over the rear suspension, Scott and Marter fabricated their own floor panel, providing some extra suspension clearance in the process.

The trunk floor was also repaired using Dennis Carpenter Ford Restoration Parts trunk panels. Since the spare tirewell was eliminated on our car, that area was filled with a flat panel while the remainder of the trunk was repaired using Dennis Carpenter Ford Restoration Parts panels trimmed to fit our rusted areas.

The new rockers and floors made the car structurally sound again, while much of this work will not show on the finished product, it is very important that it be done correctly. The final portion of the rust repair lies in the outer skin.

As it turns out we used every single piece that Dennis Carpenter Ford Restoration Parts offers for the '49-51 Ford, and that includes the two-piece lower quarter-panels. These repair panels proved to be a lifesaver for our shoebox, and while the team

at Honest Charley Garage could have fabricated these panels by hand, the labor saving from just the quarter-panels alone was immense.

Of course if you see external rust you can bet there is internal rust behind the panel. Sure enough, behind those rusted quarter-panels we found rusted wheelhouses. Panels were fabricated and welded in place on the wheelhouses before the lower quarter-panels were fitted and welded in place. One of the biggest challenges in serious rust repair is actually locating the panels when many of the mounting points have been eaten away. Much time was spent carefully measuring to be sure the panels were in the proper location.

After the rust was repaired, Marter and Scott teamed up and removed the accent spear from the quarter-panel. Finally they were out of the rust and into the fun part of modifying the car. It was a lot of work, but in the end we have the satisfaction of saving another vintage car and the team at Honest Charley Garage has the pleasure of looking at a job well done.

❯ While the body had extensive rust issues, most of the removal panels like doors and fenders were in reasonably good shape, and a coat of primer makes parts look good again.

❯ From the side it was apparent the rust had traveled well up the cowl and also on the interior toeboard of the floor.

❯ The entire floor was wafer-thin or rusted completely through. We'll remove all of the main floor section and replace it with DCFRP panels.

❯ The first order of business is to remove all of the rusted floor panels. A cut-off wheel in a die grinder made quick work of cutting the floor out.

❯ This is the lower cowl area. It is very important to restore this properly as it is a main structural point on the body. The rocker panels connect here.

❯ A bead roller was used to duplicate the rib in the toeboard portion of the front floor. Details like this make the repair look factory fresh.

❱ More surgery was required to remove the rusted area from the cowl, providing solid metal for attaching the patch panel.

❱ A 3/4-inch plywood buck was cut out to match the shape of the cowl repair, and then the 18-gauge steel was hammer formed around the buck.

❱ The toeboard panel is tack-welded in place; note the flanged outer edge that matches the factory flange on the cowl.

❱ The hammer-formed patch panel sandwiches the toeboard flange and extends down into the lower doorjamb to form the basis for the rocker panel mounting point.

❱ The toeboard is fully welded and now it is time to construct the lower cowl box and repair the upper cowl.

❱ The panel was tack-welded in place with a Millermatic 211 MIG welder and finish welded with a Miller Dynasty 200 TIG welder. A little grinding dresses off the welds.

❯ The patch panel is now complete. Once again, note how the lower portion is flanged to provide a mounting point for the rest of the lower doorjamb.

❯ Next, a small box was formed in a metal brake to construct the lower doorjamb box. This box connects to the doorjamb and to the floorboard.

❯ The final welding and grinding make the lower doorjamb as good as new and ready for the DCFRP connection.

❯ The new rocker panels are made of two pieces: the inner rocker panel, which is basically a flat filler piece; and then the formed outer rocker panel.

❯ Certain the box is in the proper size it is finished welded using the Millermatic 211. The box was built to conform to the new DCFRP outer rocker panel.

❯ The flanged inner rocker is welded in place with a series of 1/2-inch welds. Note the inner panel is flanged to fit, while the short beads in the panel add stiffness.

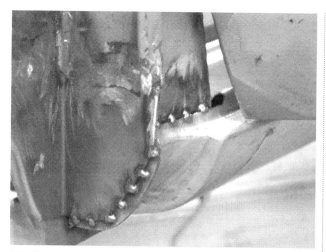

❱ The Honest Charley Garage–built lower doorjamb and the DCFRP rocker panel fit together perfectly.

❱ After lining the body mount up with the body mount holes in the Fatman Fabrications chassis, it was welded to the inner rocker panel.

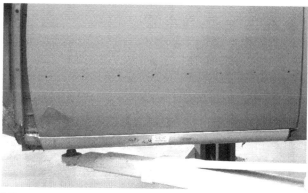

❱ The door was mounted and all gaps were checked prior to welding the rocker panel in place. This is important as once the rocker is welded in place changing the door opening is impossible.

❱ Moving to the rear, the same process was used to mount the second body mount at the base of the B-pillar. A nut was welded inside the body mount to make bolting the body in place a bit easier.

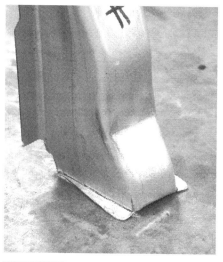

❱ Next up is installing the new DCFRP body mounts. These channel-shaped "outriggers" attach to the inner rocker panel. A small flange was hammered onto the end for a mounting surface.

❱ With the inner and outer rocker panels in place, along with the two new body mounts and reconstructed cowl, our '51 Ford is becoming structurally sound once more.

▶ The lower radius of the new rocker panel matched the roll of the quarter-panel and front fender perfectly. The rocker seams will be filled when the quarter-panels are installed.

▶ A quick test-fit of the DCFRP lower quarter-panels show they will fill the void left by rust. But first we decided to eliminate the gas filler door and the accent spear on the quarter-panel.

▶ After the rockers are in place the new floors go in quickly. The large flange on the inboard side mates to the transmission tunnel.

▶ A cut-off wheel follows the taped line to remove the unwanted metal, this modification will change the look of the quarter-panel dramatically.

▶ The rear portion of the floorboard was solid, so the rusted floor was trimmed to meet the raised portion of the rear floor. The car is being built as a "Business Sedan" so no rear seat is planned.

▶ The irregular shape of the opening will make the panel-forming process a little tricky, but Honest Charley Garage is up to the task.

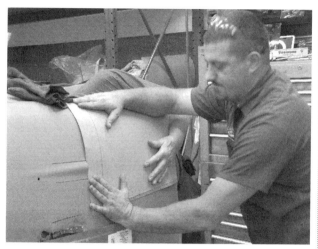

❯ The first step is to make a poster board template of the opening. By using a flexible template you will arrive at the actual size of the opening.

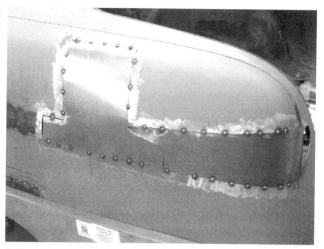

❯ After several rounds of test-fit, roll a bit more, test-fit again, the panel is trimmed and tack welded in place.

❯ The beginning of the roll was formed by simply pressing down on a piece of 6-inch pipe. Press and roll, press and roll, gently until the panel begins to take shape.

❯ When we cut all of the rust off the lower quarter-panels there was no lower quarter-panel left! And yes, the wheel houses had rusted through too.

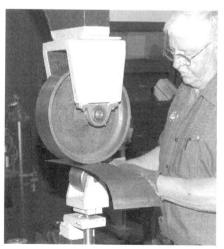

❯ After the panel has been mildly rolled Delton Scott takes the panel on the English wheel to form the compound bends required to match the quarter-panel.

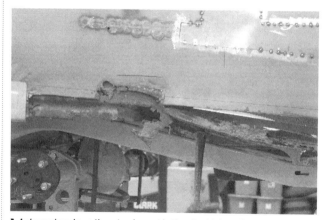

❯ A closer view shows the extensive rust in the wheel tubs and surrounding area. All of this material was removed high enough to find good metal.

❭ The rear of the wheel tub was repaired and a portion of the DCFRP rear floor was cut to fit the rusty corner on our '51 Ford. Once again, all of these pieces interconnect for strength.

❭ The lower quarter-panels were TIG-welded using a series of 1-inch welds on opposite ends of the seam to minimize warping. A Miller TIG welding unit was used.

❭ A new panel was formed and welded in place to restore the rusted wheelhouse. This panel is tied into the floor, too.

❭ Our rust had crept up well above the lower quarter-panels so a larger patch panel was formed to fill the bad area.

❭ A row of Cleco fasteners hold the DCFRP lower quarter-panels in place. The panel included the portion of the lower doorjamb but it was trimmed off for our application.

❭ The braces behind the rear wheel had rusted through so Honest Charley Garage formed a new brace. This completes the quarter-panel repair.

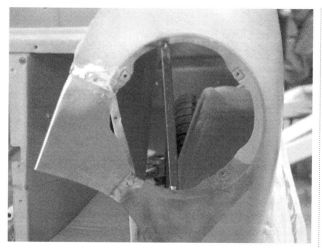

❯ The front fender had rust on the inside headlight panel. Once again a panel was formed over a plywood buck to fill the void.

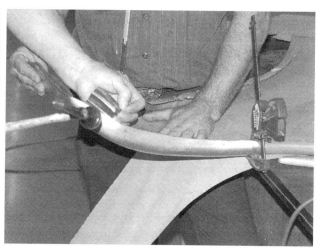

❯ The lower patch panel fits the fenderwell and some hammer and dolly work forms the leading edge to the new fender brace.

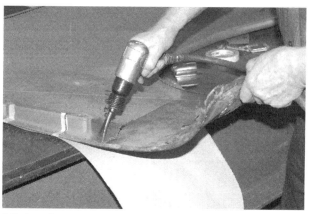

❯ The lower fender was rusted out too. An air chisel opens up the flanged area from the inner brace to the outer skin.

❯ A little heat shrinking was in order to make the leading edge of the patch panel conform to the brace. Heat, hammer, and quench to shrink it to shape.

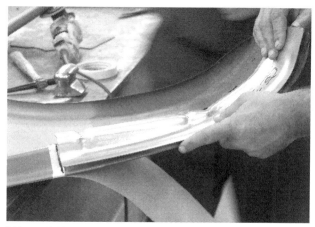

❯ The new DCFRP inner fender brace is trimmed to the point where we found good metal on our existing fender.

❯ A test-fit of the fender with the patch panel tack-welded in place allows Scott to check the lower contour with the new rocker panels. The fit was excellent.

❯ And here it is, a rust-free '51 Ford, thanks to Honest Charley Garage and Dennis Carpenter Ford Restoration Parts. Now we can begin the modification process.

HOW TO BUILD A '51 FORD ▮ 61

Dropping the Shoebox Ford Over the Frame Without Cutting the Floor

⁕ *BY GERRY BURGER* ⁕ *PHOTOGRAPHY BY THE AUTHOR* ⁕

❭ With all the rust repair out of the way it is time to start modifying the car to look like the rendering provided by Eric Black. The first step was to channel the body. We opted to "angle channel" the car, dropping it more in the rear.

Channeling a car is the simple or not-so simple act of lowering the body over the frame. This lowers both the overall profile of the car and the center of mass. It is one of the big three modifications in the hot rod and custom car world; chop, channel, and section, all different methods to achieve a lower profile. The reasons are often different for each modification, but it is safe to say that top chopping came about first as an effort to cheat the wind. By lowering the frontal area of the windshield the associated wind resistance was dropped dramatically and speeds increased. Channeling and sectioning tend to lower body roll on a car and this aids handling through curves. But for the custom crowd all of these modifications were all about restyling the car.

As most readers know, the 2013 AMSOIL/*STREET RODDER* Road Tour car is based on a '51 Ford sedan. The shoebox Ford has been a customizing favorite since 1949 and when the original car rolled into the Honest Charley Garage it also came with a great rendering by Eric Black. The rendering depicts an interesting approach to the shoebox Ford. By all rights this would be considered a radical custom, and yet the lines are so clean that it almost comes

off as a mild custom. The top will be chopped, hood will be pancaked, and all trim will be eliminated. The stance is low, with a slight tail-dragger look.

The '51 was resting on a new Fatman Fabrications chassis, which lowered the ride height considerably, but to achieve that perfect custom stance seen in the rendering would require either Z-ing the frame or channeling the body. After studying the underside of the car it became apparent that the body could be lowered down almost 3 inches without cutting the main floor of the car. Wow, what a concept: channel a car without hacking up the floors. It

> The first order of business was removing the front clip, as we would be lifting the body on and off the Fatman Fabrications frame during the channeling process.

> After raising the car, Delton Scott begins unbolting the body. Ford was serious about mounting the body in 1951 as they use no less than 16 bolts to hold the body on the frame. Notice how close the rear crossmember is to the floorpan.

may sound too good to be true, but with some careful reconfiguring of the body mounts on the frame and the body, you can actually lower the body over the frame with minimal disturbance to the main floor. You will have to cut a slot in the floor at the very rear of the trunk to allow the rear crossmember to come up flush with the floor. It should be noted that we opted to "angle channel" the '51, with no channeling at the firewall it then becoming progressively deeper channeled over each body mount as we move to the rear of the car. This angle gives us the tail-dragger stance we were looking for and it was a whole lot easier than Z-ing the frame.

Basically here is how it works: When Ford built the '51 Ford chassis they incorporated small pads or mounting brackets for the body to bolt to. This provided access to the nut and provided a platform for the rubber body mount. These brackets stand about 1-1/2 inches above the frame. On the side of the frame "outrigger" body mounts protrude and bolt to the outer rocker panel areas as the framerails ride well inside the rocker panels. Since all Fatman Fabrications chassis are designed to permit a stock body to be bolted in place, they too incorporate the body-mounting

platforms on top of the chassis and the required outer body mounts. This makes mounting any '51 Ford body to a Fatman Fabrications chassis a simple, direct bolt-on operation.

When Ford built the '51 bodies a similar body mount bracket was welded to the bottom of the floor. This floor bracket lined up with the chassis bracket and the body was bolted in place. It too protrudes down about 1 inch.

It soon became obvious that by eliminating the raised mounting pad on top of the chassis we could effectively channel the body by 1-1/2 inches. By eliminating the corresponding body mounts on the bottom of the floor we could gain another inch. Since the Fatman Fabrications chassis is built from box tubing the only modification to the frame was cutting some access holes in the side of the frame so the nut on the body bolt could be accessed. We also had to move the coilover shock mounting crossmember that was welded to the top of the frame and move it down so it was even with the top of the frame. While you don't have to cut out the floor like a more conventional channeling job, due to our four-link coilover rear suspension we did have to cut clearance holes in

the floor for the suspension brackets. If you were using the stock parallel leaf springs this crossmember would not be on the frame and the clearance holes for the four-link would not be required either, so the floor would remain intact. For that reason if you're planning on channeling your body over a Fatman Fabrications frame it may be easier to simply order the chassis with stock-style rear leaf springs.

Working at Honest Charley Garage made this process easier because their state-of-the-art shop includes a lift. By using the lift the body could easily be raised off the frame and then lowered back down for test-fitting, and there is a lot of test-fitting.

As we removed the chassis body mounts and lowered the car down it became apparent that we would have to remove a section from the new Dennis Carpenter Ford Restoration Parts body mounts that we had welded in place while repairing the extensive rust in the car. This was a simple matter of cutting a section out of the bottom of the mount and then welding the lower piece back onto the upper portion of the bracket. We cut a little extra out of these body mounts, as you can always shim the body back up but you sure can't shim something down!

❯ The Fatman Fabrications chassis employs the same style body mount as the original '51 Ford. The raised platform-style body mounts will be cut off the frame to channel the body down over the frame. The raised body mounts on the body will also be removed.

❯ The rear outrigger mount is shorter and deeper than the front mount. We will section the rear mount 1/2-inch deeper than the front mount to achieve the desired angle on the channeling job.

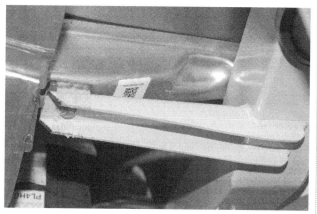

❯ These outriggers on the chassis reach out to the factory body mounts that are located just inside the rocker panels. The new body mounts are from Dennis Carpenter Ford Restoration Parts. We'll section the body mount to lower the body.

❯ As you can see the Fatman frame drops the rear of the car, but we need to find several more inches to achieve that cool, down-in-the-back custom look in the rendering.

We now had the body resting on the framerails, but the brackets were still on the floorpan. This dropped the car a little more than an inch and while that may not sound like much, the difference in profile was both noticeable and remarkable.

At this point we could have settled for a moderate channel and never fired up our Miller Plasma cutter. But to be true to the rendering we required a deeper channel so we moved onto removing the body mounts that are welded to the bottom of the floor.

A die grinder and cut-off wheel made short work of removing the mounts. Once again the body was lowered down to check for clearance. At this point we were getting very close to the top of the center X-member on the Fatman frame and we knew we must have a gap between the top of the frame and the body.

Next we removed a strip from the very rear of the trunk floor. This allowed the body to slide down over the rear crossmember. For some reason we forgot or missed the second to last set of body mounts on the floorpan and that turned out to be a good thing. By leaving them intact the body was down to within less than 1/2 inch of the top of the frame but still gave us the 2-3/4-inch drop (at the rear pan) we were hoping for.

After some shimming and measuring we had dropped the car on a very pleasing front to the rear angle with minimal invasion of the floorpan. Mounting the rear bumper will require some custom mounts and sheetmetal work but the overall effect is very rewarding. As the profile on our '51 Ford goes down, the cool factor goes up.

For a better understanding of how the entire process works let's follow along with the team at Honest Charley Garage as they channel the shoebox and save the floor.

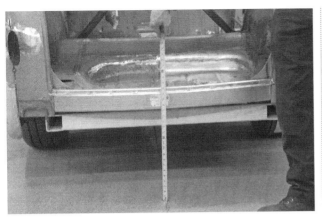

❯ Our baseline measurement shows 17-1/2 inches to the bottom of the rear pan, which by the way is another DCFRP replacement panel. After channeling this pan was dropped 2-3/4 inches.

❯ The last body mount in the rear of the car is located in the back corner. This area of the floor will be notched to allow the body to drop over the rear crossmember.

❯ Because we wanted the improved handling provided by QA1 coilover shocks we will have to notch the floor to clear the associated four-link brackets. Delton Scott marks the area to be removed for clearance.

❯ Richard Marter drills through the floor using the frame mount as a guide to properly locate the hole. The stock rubber body insulators will be used between the modified mounts and the floor.

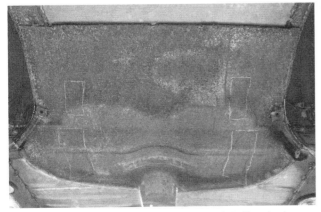

❯ After marking the bottom side of the floor in all areas that will require clearance, the body was lifted off the frame.

❯ With the body off the frame it is time to remove and relocate the rear crossmember. Note the raised pads atop the framerails that serve as body mounts.

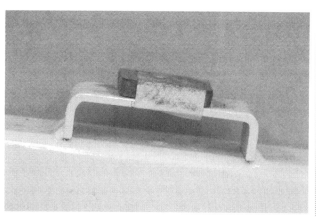

❱ Looking from the side, it becomes obvious that we can lower the body 1-1/2 inches by simply removing the stock-style body mounts from the top of the rails.

❱ After trimming the crossmember to move down and to the rear, we fired up the trusty Millermatic and welded the crossmember in its new location.

❱ Working in a state-of-the-art shop like Honest Charley Garage has its benefits, such as this lift. Using the lift to raise and lower the body makes life easy, but this job could be done at home with jacks as well.

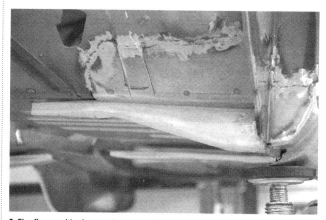

❱ The floor and body mounts were replaced with parts from DCFRP. This front mount will now be sectioned 3/4 inch to lower the body.

❱ Marter takes the cut-off wheel to the welds around the rear crossmember, in the process removing and relocating the crossmember.

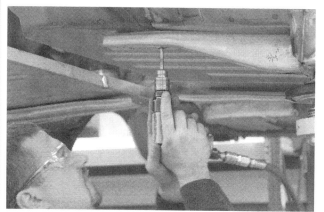

❱ Prior to modifying the mount we drilled the inboard body mounting hole up through the floor. This will ensure perfect alignment later.

❱ After carefully marking the cut lines with a square we cut the bottom section out of the mount. Team Honest Charley Garage will fabricate new flat bottoms for the mounts.

❱ Here we can see both the front and rear side body mounts have been notched in the channeling process. We cut the notches deeper than the actual channel depth to allow for some body shimming later.

❱ This is the modified rear mount. You will notice the end of the mount has also been trimmed to provide clearance between the top of the X-member and the new, lower floorpan.

❱ Simple pieces of 1/8-inch flat stock were cut to fit the opening and then MIG-welded in place to form the new mount. A nut is welded to the inside of the plate to receive the body bolt in the blind body mount. Note the factory rubber insulator being used.

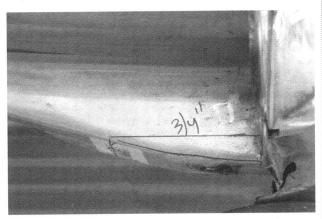

❱ The front mount will be modified with a similar cut. We will remove 3/4 inch up front as the channeling depth is less up front.

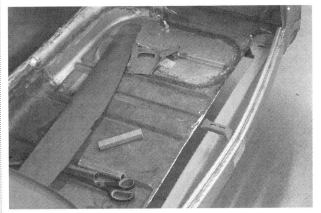

❱ The rearmost section of the trunk floor was neatly cut out with a Miller plasma cutter to allow the rear crossmember to come up even with the trunk floor. After trimming the crossmember to move down and to the rear, we fired up the trusty Millermatic and welded the crossmember in its new location.

❱ A piece of 1/8-inch plate was fabricated with the proper body mounting holes drilled. This stout piece of metal makes for one very solid body mount, and once again the stock rubber insulators are used between the body and frame.

❱ Looking at the rear of the car it is clear we have gained a lot of lowering. The rear pan is now almost even with the bottom of the rear crossmember.

❱ With the body back on the frame we can see the number of holes required to clear the four-link. Since this is going to be a "business sedan" with no back seat, a new floor section was planned.

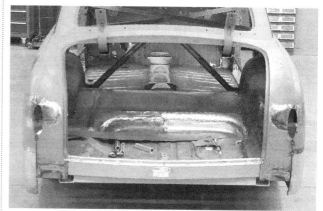

❱ Looking from the trunk forward the main floorpan is completely intact, something you seldom see on a channeled car.

❱ The raised floor will provide plenty of room for Jerry Dixey to carry his wares and it also provided lots of room for suspension travel. If desired, a seat could be mounted to this raised floor.

❱ This side profile tells it all, notice how the top of the rear wheel opening is now level with the top lug nut. Before the channeling that same lip was well above the hubcap lip. The angle channeling made a dramatic difference in the profile and mood of our '51 Ford.

❯ One look at the Eric Black rendering and you can see Honest Charley Garage is well on the way to matching the rendering.

The Road Tour Car Goes Low Profile

✳ BY GERRY BURGER ✳ PHOTOGRAPHY BY THE AUTHOR ✳

❭ *The car has been channeled on a slight angle to the rear. With no channeling at the firewall and 3 inches in the rear, this gives it that slight tail-dragger look. Our top chop will be 2 inches at the A-pillar and 3-1/2 inches at the rear window to continue the angular stance.*

The '49-51 shoebox Ford derives its nickname from the somewhat slab-sided appearance that gives the car that iconic boxy look. These were the first new bodies from Ford after World War II and the rear fenders had melted into the quarter-panels, the front fenders had risen to meet the hood, and they too were now flush with the doors. There wasn't so much as a hint of a running board and grille openings were lower and wider than ever before. By 1949 standards it was quite a modern approach to the automobile and that style would endure for three years.

All this modern sleekness made a perfect canvas for customizers and not long after these cars arrived at the local Ford dealer hot rodders and customizers were modifying these smooth new automobiles. Terms like chop, channel, and section were applied to these new cars and suddenly a sleek car became downright slippery.

And so 64 years later we're still reshaping the shoebox. Eric Black provided the team at Honest Charley Garage with a rendering that employs all of the time-tested modifications but still has managed to create a look that is traditional, fresh, and restrained. We're about to chop the car 2 inches up front and 3-1/2 in the back, and then we'll pancake the hood. All very traditional modifications to produce a custom of perfect proportions.

One of the more interesting features on the AMSOIL/*STREET RODDER* Road Tour car is while the car has the look of a radical custom, none of the modifications required to achieve that profile would be considered radical. Chopping the shoebox Ford 2 inches is conservative by any measure and likewise channeling the car was also limited to a few inches. And yet, in combination the profile is somehow radically lowered without putting painful restrictions on the interior space, something Jerry Dixey will be pleased to hear. As a matter of fact, when the Wiseguys seats are installed the view out of the chopped windshield will be straight forward, with no need for

❱ The side windows on a '51 Ford sedan are nearly the same size and it gives the car a certain old, stodgy sedan attitude. Dropping the top will shorten the rear window a bit and give it a more interesting shape.

❱ With the roof down to bare metal it's time to start measuring, marking, and thinking about where to cut the top for the best results. Best results always involve minimal cutting.

❱ Greg Cunningham and Tommy Lee Byrd man the DA sanders to remove all of the protective primer from the roof area. This will ensure good, clean MIG and TIG welds from our Miller Electric Mfg. Co. welders.

❱ The team at Honest Charley Garage has laid out the center line on the roof, the cut line on the panel in front of the decklid, and the cut lines on the A- and B-pillars.

hunching over for a clear view of the road.

Chopping any postwar car brings challenges that require excellent and advanced sheetmetal forming skills. The compound curves, the overall size of the panels, and the curved rear glass all present challenges to overcome. If chopping a Model T coupe is a 1, lowering the lid on a shoebox would come in around an 8.

However, the principles remain the same; think before you cut, measure, mark, and then measure and mark again before you do any cutting. Taking a side, front, and rear photograph and doing a "paper chop" is a good way to anticipate problem areas. Finally, always try to make each cut precise and clean. You'll be glad you did later when it comes time to fit those panels back together.

One problem area on any top chop is the rear corner of the quarter window. In stock form the lower rear corner of the quarter glass incorporates a pleasing radius and it is important to maintain a radius and avoid the dreaded "pinched corner" seen on poorly executed chops. Another major decision involves dealing with the rain gutter or driprail. On most cars the driprail not only channels water away from the top of the door, it is also a feature line of the car. Removing the driprail can make a roof look altogether too round and will also allow water to freely

enter the top of the doors. Once again if removing the driprail is part of your plan, try doing it on a photograph first and remember you will also have to seal the doors properly. Finally there is the vent window issue. While it is popular to remove the vent window, bear in mind it can make the door glass look excessively long, and possibly more importantly it can make fitting roll-up glass a real problem.

As it turns out our Eric Black illustration included both a pleasant rear radius, driprail retention, and maintaining the vent wing window at the A-pillar. All three of these decisions by the artist keep the car flowing and traditional in appearance.

After spending hours measuring, marking, taping, and pondering, Delton Scott and Richard Marter plugged in the Sawzall and connected the cut-off wheels. The relatively mild 2-inch chop will minimize misalignment of the top and bottom but there is still plenty of work to do. Bear in mind that the more you remove, the greater the disparity in panel alignment. The amount of work in a 2-inch chop is dramatically less than the work encountered for a 4- or 5-inch chop, something to remember when you are contemplating lowering any lid.

Prior to beginning the chop, the entire interior of the car must be crossbraced, which means door openings and across the B-pillars and even putting a couple of braces in the rear window opening to preserve that shape. When installing your bracing you must make it substantial enough to hold the body in shape but also allow enough room to crawl inside because there will be some inside work during the top chopping process.

Key measurements and marks include a perfect centerline on the roof with a corresponding center line on the cowl and the rear panel in front of the decklid. If any cuts are at all confusing, simple notes and arrows written on the top with a Sharpie will help avoid cutting "on the wrong side of the line." In short, take your time and think things through.

After removing all paint from the roof, any trace of a headliner, and all interior moldings, we were ready to begin the top chop. Cutting began at the A-pillars, then moved to the rear roof area, followed by the final cuts at the B-pillar. From here it is easier to illustrate the process through the accompanied photos and captions so follow along as we drop the top on our '51 Ford AMSOIL/ *STREET RODDER* Road Tour car.

❱ A 2-inch chop is pretty conservative on a shoebox Ford, but it had a surprisingly large impact on the profile of the car, sometimes more isn't better. Whenever possible use tape to mark cut lines. This minimizes the chances of mismeasuring.

❱ The center line is marked on the roof and also on the panel in front of the decklid. The lower band of yellow tape is the cut line to free the rear window from the body. Note the braces in the rear window.

❱ The first cut and most import piece to preserve is the lower rear corner of the rear side glass. This panel will be removed to save the curved rear corner.

❱ A Sawzall is best for cutting through the multiple layers of steel that make up the window frame area. Work slowly and make your cuts clean and perfectly on the mark.

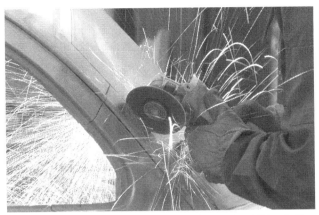

❯ A cut-off wheel is used to cut through the single-layer steel roof. This cut will free the window corner from the body.

❯ After removing the lower corner of the window opening you have a gaping hole, but you will be glad you cut this piece out later in the process.

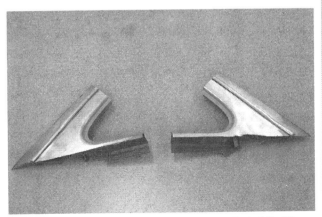

❯ After doing both sides you should have a couple of pieces that look like this. Measuring and making cuts the exact same on each side will help to ensure perfect window symmetry when lowering the top.

❯ Next Richard Marter uses a cut-off wheel to slice through the upper portion of the roof. Be careful not to get too close to the bracing around the rear window, as roof material will be removed later and you may need to do some hammer and dolly work there, too.

❯ With the rear roof portion cut we move up front to the A-pillar. Once again the Sawzall makes quick work of cutting the pillar, carefully making a square cut.

❯ Now is a good time to buy a pizza and have a bunch of friends over to the house: lifting the roof off is a four-man job. If Editor Brennan is one of the guys lifting, better order an extra pizza.

❱ At this point you are experiencing pride and fear at the same instance. Sure you're a real man who just cut the roof off a perfectly good car, but now are you man enough to put it back on?

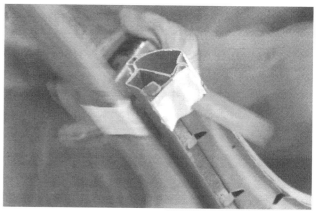

❱ Now the pillars can be cut. Always cut the top free first, then make the secondary cuts on the pillar stubs, as that is much easier than trying to hold the top and cut the posts.

❱ The door tops, rear roof section, and all of those posts sure look strange sticking up in the air.

❱ Moving to the rear, the B-pillar receives a similar cut with the Sawzall. Save every piece that is removed as these pieces will form filler pieces later and they have all the right profiles.

❱ The original rear window is curved glass and for that reason it will remain uncut. While that big window looks huge now, when it is laid forward it will appear dramatically smaller.

❱ Once again it's all hands on deck to lift the top into place for the first test-fit after cutting the posts down 2 inches. This is the first check of misalignment.

❯ The front A-pillars had minimal misalignment. Since the cuts were made in the straightest area of the posts it will be a simple job of pulling the lower posts inward for alignment.

❯ After cutting both A-pillars a cargo strap was used to pull the two posts together to align them with the top. If the posts don't align, more material may need to be removed from the A-pillar cut.

❯ As the top moves forward to meet the new, lower A-pillar the B-pillar will also misalign. This misalignment is pretty minimal as top chops go and will be simple to remedy.

❯ After pulling the bottom posts together with the cargo strap the angle cuts in the A-pillar are perfectly closed when the lower posts and roof posts are aligned.

❯ The top is lifted off and the trusty Sawzall makes an angle cut at the bottom radius of the A-pillar. The required cut was just 1/8 inch.

❯ Satisfied with the post alignment we gave them several good tack welds using our Millermatic MIG welder.

❱ Since the B-pillar is actually holding the top in place a brace was fabricated from box tubing to hold the top in position while we align the two posts.

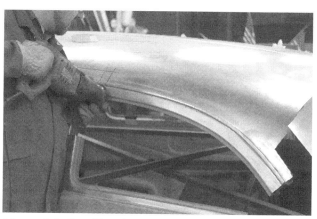

❱ Once again the Sawzall is used to cut through any areas where there are multiple layers and again work slowly to keep your cuts perfectly straight on the line.

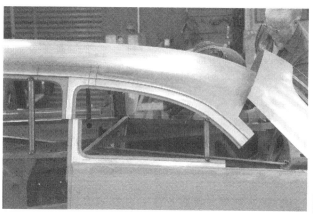

❱ With the roof braced we can begin work on the B-pillar, and you can't help but notice what appears to be a huge misalignment at the rear of the roof.

❱ The cut-off wheel makes a clean cut through the roof skin to free the B-pillar from the roof.

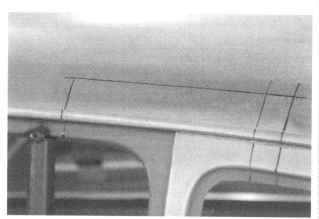

❱ We carefully marked out the cut on the roof. Basically we are cutting the B-pillar free from the roof and moving it rearward. The small box marked at the rear of the cut lines is the amount that the post must be moved to the rear.

❱ With the B-pillar free from the roof we will remove a section off the back of the piece we cut out so it can move to the rear. The piece we cut off the back will be used to fill the void in the front.

❱ After cutting the proper amount of the rear of the upper B-pillar piece we clamped the shortened piece in place to align it with the lower B-pillar stub.

❱ The B-pillars are aligned, now we must fill the void in front of the relocated piece. The piece that was removed from the rear of the upper B-pillar will fill the void perfectly.

❱ Satisfied with the B-pillar alignment we tack-welded the pillars together and tack-welded the roof skin back together, too.

❱ Here we can see the piece that was removed from the rear of the upper pillar is now tack-welded in place on the roof. Notice the driprails are also tack-welded and aligned at this time.

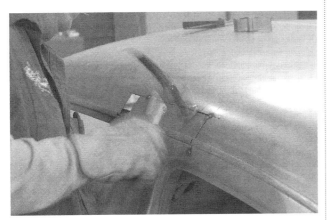

❱ After tack-welding the piece in place, Delton Scott used the Eastwood hammer and dolly to massage the metal into perfect alignment.

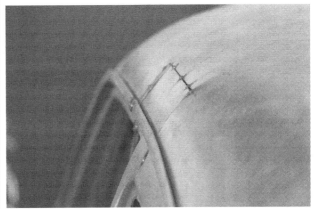

❱ Check your work as you go and check it from all angles to be certain all the sheetmetal is flowing smoothly and is devoid of any unwanted bumps, lumps, or waves.

❱ Now for the scary part, aligning the rear window area with the roof. While this looks pretty daunting, laying the window forward will close the gap considerably.

❱ Leaning the rear window forward requires that we cut it free from the panel between the window and the decklid. A cut-off wheel handles the job and once again stays true to the line.

❱ Those package shelf braces serve as a telescoping set of brackets to clamp the roof in place for alignment. The roof is moved forward 3 inches and leaned downward.

❱ The final cuts are inside the window through the package shelf braces. Measure and mark the cuts square so you can use them as references when aligning the roof.

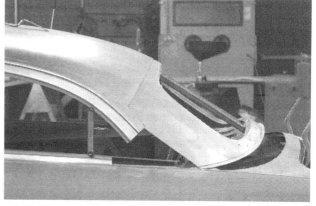

❱ And just like that the huge gap has closed up. This lowered the roof 3-1/2-inches in the rear, on a more radical chop the roof skins would need to be reshaped.

❱ With the rear window leaning forward the glass area appears smaller and there will have to be a little bit of panel stretching on the outer ends of the window panel.

❱ Looking from the rear we can see the misalignment on the rear sides of the window panel. Since the roof pieces are overlapped by 3 inches we marked the rear roof area and carefully cut the excess off.

❱ Before we aligned the two pieces of roof skin an Eastwood little hammer and dolly were used in order to gently lift the ends of the main roof skin.

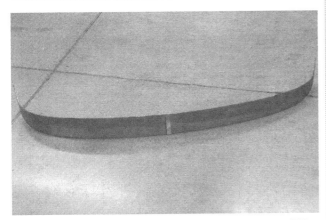

❱ Here is the piece we removed; it was attached to the rear window panel. With this piece removed the two roof skins will butt up to each other.

❱ We used our Eastwood hammer and dolly to gently lower the end of the roof skin above the rear window. By moving the main skin up and the rear skin down we achieved perfect alignment.

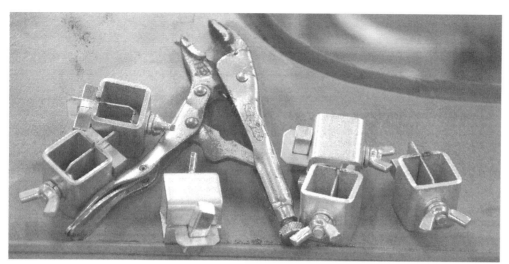

❱ Aligning two long panels requires a lot of Eastwood panel clamps. One lesson here, don't scrimp on these clamps. The closer the clamps, the better the alignment.

❱ As we worked from the center out, the Eastwood panel clamps pulled the two skins into perfect alignment. Note that the center lines are also perfectly matched on the roof panels.

❱ Next Richard Marter fired up the Millermatic and put a tack-weld between each clamp, moving from side to side to minimize any heat distortion.

❱ We worked the panel clamps down around the corners of the roof and all that sheetmetal was gently moving into place.

❱ With the roof skin tack welded between the clamps, our '51 Ford was looking like a car once more. A bit more hammer and dolly work will perfect the roof skin contour.

❱ Once again we took the time to "eyeball" all the angles and curves on the roof to be certain we had a nice flowing top line. One look from this angle tells you it just doesn't get any better than this.

❱ We used a cut-off wheel to cut through the overlapped package tray brackets and then welded them solid with our Millermatic MIG welder.

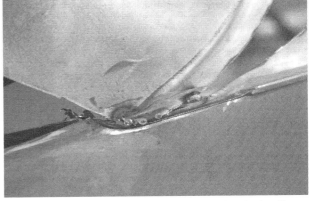

❱ The roof was now attached to the body through a series of solid tack welds, including down at the corners where the roof meets the quarter-panels.

❱ After making a cardboard template for the required filler panel the shape was transferred to some 18-gauge sheet steel.

❱ After carefully fitting the filler panel it was clamped into place with Eastwood panel clamps. This filler piece visually lengthens the trunk area, which takes that "grandma's sedan" look out of the car.

❱ Using an Eastwood hammer and dolly it took some work on the edges but in the end the filler panel fit perfectly. The formed filler panel is held in alignment for welding using Eastwood panel clamps.

❱ Once again a series of tack-welds connect the filler panel to the rear window and to the decklid area. At this point the roof is one with the body again.

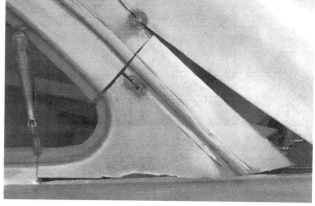

❱ Often this rear radius will have to be closed up by pie-cutting the piece and folding it closed, but in this case we managed to use the stock radius on the rear window corner for a real factory look.

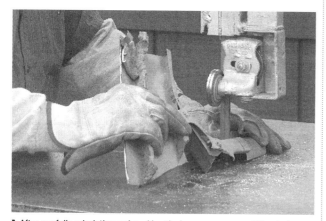

❱ After carefully calculating and marking the lower rear corners of the window, Delton Scott cuts the top and bottom ends off the window radius piece that we removed earlier.

❱ Satisfied with the fit of the lower window piece, Marter tack-welds the piece in place.

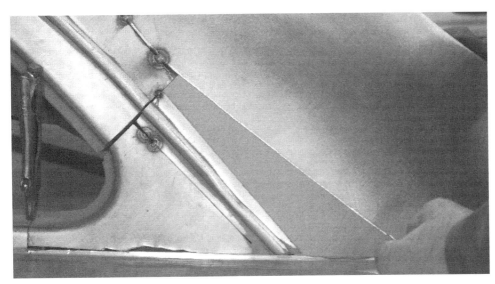

❱ After tack welding the window corner in place it was time to make a filler piece for the sail panel behind the window. First the opening was trimmed to a uniform shape that eliminated the sharp point at the top of the panel.

❱ While the filler panel is small it does carry a compound curve. Scott uses the English wheel to form that curve. This same curve could be formed with a shot bag and mallet by the homebuilder.

❱ We were truly pleased with the smooth flowing lines of the rear window area and after some final welding and sanding of the welds there will be nearly no filler required on the seams.

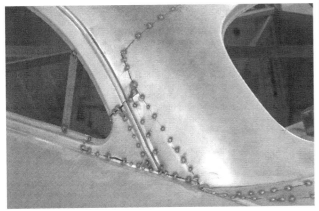

❱ After some careful grinding and fitting the final filler piece was tack-welded into the roof. Notice how well the panels fit and more importantly notice how few cuts were made to the roof. This is the reward of good craftsmanship and restraint when lowering the lid.

❱ We couldn't be happier with the shape of the rear window. It is shorter so it has a bit more of a coupe look and that rear corner radius is perfect. The small brace showing in the window is temporary.

❯ The extended area between the decklid and the rear window visually lengthens our '51 Ford, and while the rear window is still original size it appears smaller on this angle.

❯ With the top lowered, team Honest Charley Garage turned their attention to lowering the doorframes.

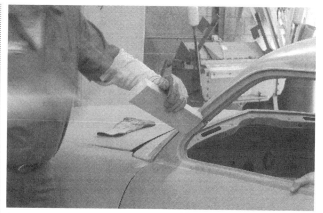

❯ For the most part this top chop was a gentle operation with minimal force exerted, but sometimes there is just no substitute for a 2x4 and a hammer to move a post in 1/8 inch.

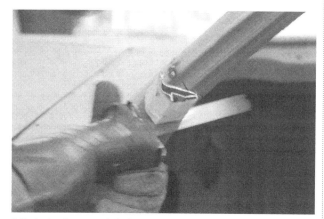

❯ The basic cuts were made in the same places as the main roof cuts, which helps ensure symmetry between the upper door and the now lowered roof.

❯ The window frame portion of the door was cut in the center to allow the front and rear pieces to align properly. Since we moved the B-pillar to the rear we will need to add a filler piece to the top of the door.

❯ Remember those pieces you cut out of the B-pillar to lower the roof? Simply trim one of those to fit the void in the middle of the upper door.

❯ The inside window moldings were also cut to fit the new window opening, which means they too were lowered and extended to fit the opening.

❯ The rear window frame was carefully fit to the reshaped rear side window, including moving the lower rear radius a bit. It is important that these fit perfectly as they help retain the window rubber.

❯ The front vent window post was trimmed and reinstalled in the door. We like the look of the vent window as it visually shortens the door glass area. The vents will fold out and work just like they did in 1951.

❯ And here it is, the 2013 AMSOIL/STREET RODDER Road Tour car with an all-new low profile. We were amazed at what a dramatic difference removing only 2 inches from the front and 3-1/2 inches from the rear made on the overall profile, proving you don't have to go radical to achieve a great look.

Flawless Paint and Brilliant Chrome

✳ *BY RON CERIDONO AND GERRY BURGER* ✳ *PHOTOGRAPHY BY GERRY BURGER* ✳

❱ *The 2013 AMSOIL/STREET RODDER Road Tour Ford gleams thanks to the PPG paint applied by Honest Charley Garage and the flawless chrome by Sherm's Custom Plating.*

From the beginning of the program Road Tour cars have been built to be driven, but fit and finish have always been equally important. Thanks to the crew at Honest Charley Garage that tradition continues. Our Ford is ready to gobble up the miles and look great doing it.

With any street rod project, including our Road Tour cars, we can think of no single day more exciting than laying down the final finish. The hundreds of hours of metalwork, hammering, blocking, and sanding all culminate with the careful mixing and applying of the final paint. It's a glory day, the one that brings out the personality of the car, and in the world of hot rods paint has very little to do with protection from the elements and everything to do about making a statement. Because of that, color choice is one of the most critical and difficult decisions to make during a build. Pick a cool color that works with the car and you've got a winner; pick the wrong color for the car and regardless of how good the workmanship and selected modifications may be the car will never look "right."

Luckily we had three things going for us: Eric Black's rendering was done in gold, so we immediately limited our selection to the gold family. Second, we had the great PPG Vibrance palette. Finally, we had years of experience working for us at Honest Charley Garage, and after several hours of thought,

holding color swatches inside the building, out in the sun, in the shade, and even in dim evening light, Greg Cunningham made the final call. The color would be Code 908324, Golden Dream. The finish was achieved by using a waterborne EnvroBase pearl followed by a gold midcoat over the base, followed by three coats of PPG clear.

Before the car could be painted, conventional bodywork methods were employed. PPG DF 700 premium filler was used to straighten welded seams and cover hammer and dolly marks, followed by JP 205 primer. Inside the car Eastwood seam sealer was used over the repaired floor seams. After blocking with an array

❯ While all the metalwork that had been done on our '51 Ford was near perfect, body filler was used on the minor imperfections. Spreading with a wide "bondo spreader" keeps the filler applied evenly.

❯ Long contoured panels should always be sanded with long flexible sanding blocks. Eastwood handled a complete line of sanding blocks and boards in both flexible design and stiff boards.

❯ PPG's DF700 Technifill is formulated for use with contemporary refinishing products and is used with DF708 cream hardener. DF700 spreads extremely well and sands easily.

❯ There seems to be an Eastwood sanding block for every contour on the car and that sure made sanding the car easier and more precise. From the super long-blocks to the colorful contour package they worked great.

of Eastwood sanding blocks, several coats of K36 urethane primer were laid down using an Eastwood spray gun. More sanding followed and when the body was deemed ready for paint, hours of careful cleaning masking ensued. Then it was time to start spraying. Ben Giuilano has done plenty of custom painting and has a lot of experience with waterborne paints so he was a natural to be behind the spray gun. We won't go into all the grizzly details here, but the paints were very carefully mixed, exactly as prescribed by PPG. These modern paints aren't like the lacquers of old where you mix thinners by eye. No, this is more like being a chemist; so much care is taken in mixing the paint. From there it was a matter of donning the proper safety equipment and laying down the three stages of paint. It is imperative to leave time between the coats for the paint to dry and "off gas." Allowing the vapors to

escape will prevent potential problems on the following coats. Always follow the instructions carefully, and when in doubt ask questions before you apply the paint. Your local PPG jobber is a wealth of knowledge and if they can't answer your question they can find a specialist who can. Remember, this paint isn't cheap, so getting it right the first time is imperative.

First the car was "jambed," meaning we painted inside the fenders, the doorjambs, and trunkjambs. Then the body was completely assembled and shimmed to the final fit before it was rolled into the spray booth for the topcoats. Painting the car completely assembled assures color uniformity. We've all seen cars that were painted in pieces, having color variations. Those color variations can be caused by different spray gun angles, air pressures, temperatures, and any number of seemingly minor variables. At Honest Charley Garage they have found the best way to ensure color uniformity is to paint the car assembled.

After the paint was allowed to cure overnight, the color-sanding portion of the paintjob began. The ultimate final finish is only as good as the color sanding and buffing, so the progressively finer grits of wet sandpaper were used until it was sanded to an astounding 5,000-grit finish. That's a far cry from the 600-grit we used to use on lacquer. At this point the paint is actually beginning to shine just from the fine sanding. Buffing follows using the 3M Perfect-It products and following the instructions provided with the product. After the desired luster is achieved, final cleanup is done with a good spray detailer, and the paint is finally finished with a good coat of wax.

The results speak for themselves; not only is gold the right color for this car, this is the right gold for this car. The pearl base "flops hard," meaning the color in the highlighted area, caused by either sunlight or indoor light, bursts into a brilliant gold with dazzling pearl, while the portions of the body not in direct light reflect a more subdued color. It is this contrast in light reflection that makes candy apple and pearl paints so attractive and seductive. There is simply no other final finish that can provide that look. Laying down a great paintjob takes training, talent, and time. There is simply no substitute for experience, and there is only one way to get experience, and that's by doing it. Should you elect to paint your hot rod at home, remember these important things. First and foremost: safety, use the very best paint protection. Second, a steady supply of clean dry air from your compressor, a quality spray gun, and a surgically clean spray area. Allow plenty of time to get the job done; rushing and custom painting just don't go together.

Regardless of whether you decide to tackle this job yourself or have a pro shop do it for you, follow along with the photos of our 2013 AMSOIL/*STREET RODDER* Road Tour car as we apply the finally candy gold finish. We have listed the materials of Honest Charley Garage, The Eastwood Company, and the PPG paint products to guide you in selecting the right products for your project.

Steps and PPG Materials for Paint and Bodywork

Paint Color:
908324 Golden Dream, Vibrance Collection

The following PPG Products were used to produce the final finish:
- DX1791 wash primer on bare metal after sanding with a DA to promote adhesion of the epoxy primer to bare metal
- DP40LF corrosion-resistant epoxy primer to prevent rusting during fab work
- DF700 premium body filler
- JP205 (Shop line brand of PPG) polyester primer used for high build dry sanding
- DF715 Techniglaze polyester glazing putty
- K36 urethane primer surfacer as final primer followed by wet sanding
- ECS6 sealer use for color holdout with EnviroBase paints
- EHP (EnviroBase High Performance) waterborne basecoat/midcoat
- DCU2021 clearcoat

Process:

- Finish bodywork in 150-grit and spray four coats of JP 205 primer
- Sanded JP 205 with 80-grit and finished to 220-grit, followed by three coats of K36 primer
- Sanded K36 with 400-grit and 600-grit wet
- Sealed car with one coat ECS6 sealer
- Sprayed five coats of EnviroBase pearl base color with proper flash time between coats
- Sprayed two coats of gold midcoat with proper flash time between coats
- Let set overnight (approximately 10 hours) then sprayed three coats of DCU2021 clear

Steps and Materials for Color Sanding and Buffing:

- First: Wet sanding with 1,000-grit
- Second: Wet sanding with 1,500-grit
- Third: Wet sanding with 3,000-grit
- Final: Wet sanding with 5,000-grit
- Buffing and Polishing: Recommended polisher speed is 1,200-2,000 rpm

1. Compound: 3M Perfect-It Rubbing Compound (PN 06085/06086)
   Use Foam compounding pad (PN 05706)

2. Machine Polish: 3M Perfect-It Machine Polish (PN 06064/06065)
   Use foam polishing pad (PN 05707)
   Wipe with yellow detail cloth (PN 06016)

3. Swirl Elimination: 3M Perfect-It Ultrafine Machine Polish (PN 06068/06069)
   Use foam polishing pad (PN 05708)
   Wipe with blue detail cloth (PN 06020)

4. Final clean up with a good spray detailer

5. Apply a coat of your favorite wax to protect the finish

Eastwood Tools and Equipment for Final Finish

- Hammers and dollies
- Sanding blocks
- Rolled sandpaper
- Pre-pre-paint cleaner
- Spray gun
- Body seam sealer
- Undercoating
- 2K chassis black (wheelwells)

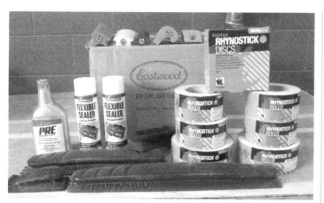

❯ Eastwood supplied a full selection of contoured, profile, and flat sanding blocks and boards. Since the sanding blocks come in such varied lengths, sandpaper is now best purchased in rolls (also from Eastwood), allowing you to fit the paper to any sanding block.

❯ An Eastwood HVLP (high-volume, low-pressure) spray gun was used to apply all the PPG products. These guns are extremely efficient as the low-pressure operation results in minimal over-spray.

❯ After the body filler was sanded to a 120-grit finish, Ben Giuilano lays down the first coat or JP 205 primer over the body filler.

❯ PPG's K36 is an excellent fast-build primer surfacer that can be easily block sanded to make body panels laser straight.

❯ The task of sanding areas such as doorjambs can be tedious but oh-so important in the finished product. Like all good bodywork it takes time and patience.

❯ Eastwood's Ceramic Chassis Black was used on the frame's center crossmember and the wheelwells.

❱ To protect the bottom of the body it was thoroughly covered with Eastwood's undercoating.

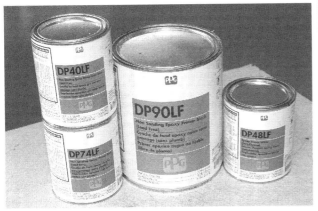

❱ PPG's DP series epoxy primer comes in a variety of colors, including green, red, black, and white.

❱ PPG's Envirobase line of products produces fabulous results without the VOC emissions that were once a by-product of refinishing.

❱ For that mile-deep look PPG offers a variety of clears that provide gloss, UV protection, and resistance to chipping.

❱ After wet sanding the JP 205 primer to 220-grit, Giuilano laid down three coats of PPG K36 primer; this would be the final coats of primer on the car.

❱ The PPG K36 primer was sanded to a 400-grit finish and then the car was "jambed," the process of spraying finish paint in the doorjambs and trunk driprails. Then the car was completely re-taped with clean paper and tape.

❱ Gone are the days of simply pouring some thinner in the paint. Today's paint requires precision mixing and the pro shops use a scale to weight each component. This is the waterborne pearl basecoat being mixed.

❱ Next up we mixed the gold midcoat. Like any candy finish the paint consists of a base, transparent color, and a topcoat clear. While this paint looks almost black, it sprays gold.

❱ Stirring the EnviroBase High Performance waterborne pearl basecoat shows the contrasting colors in the pearl that make the Vibrance paint so vibrant.

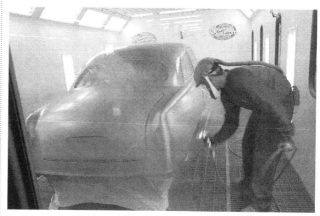

❱ Giuilano mans the spray gun and once again uniformity is the key to a great candy job. Air pressure, distance from the panel, and crossing patterns are all used to prevent dreaded stripes in the paint.

❱ After very carefully tacking and blowing the car perfectly clean, five coats of base were applied. Giuilano was very careful with air pressure settings and crossing spray patterns to provide a perfectly uniform basecoat.

❱ Ah yes, and finally it's glory time. Laying down three coats of PPG DCU 2021 clear puts on the shine and makes the color pop. This makes the hundreds of hours of bodywork all worthwhile.

❱ The final finish is flawless. It was allowed to cure for 24 hours before color sanding. It looks great in the booth, but after a couple days of color sanding and buffing the paint will really shine.

❱ An air-powered DA was used on the large flat panels, although on darker colors all sanding is done by hand. Hand sanding all the way down to a 5,000-grit was done in the tight spots. This is key to a perfect finish.

❱ Here we can see the 1,500-grit sanded quarter-panel perfectly straight and completely free of any orange peel. It would be sanded twice more before buffing.

❱ After a day or two of buffing, polishing, glazing, and finally waxing this is what the car looked like on the day of the unveiling in the Coker Tire Museum. A huge crowd was on hand to see the car, thanks to a debut cruise-in connected with the Power Tour. A tired but proud team, Honest Charley Garage, stands behind the car they built.

They say all that glitters is not gold, and in the case of the AMSOIL/*STREET RODDER* Road Tour Ford, if it's not gold, it's chrome by Sherm's Custom Plating.

What it Takes to get Perfect Plating

When it comes to the appearance of our Road Tour cars one of the elements that always stands out is the chrome, and for outstanding results we turn to Sherm's Custom Plating in Sacramento, California.

While all chrome shops use the same basic plating process, how parts are prepped has a huge impact on the finished product, just as it does with paint. In fact Art Holman of Sherm's compares chrome plating to a paintjob. In both cases the finished product is only as smooth as the surface below, and the smoother the surface the more reflective it will be. And again like a paintjob, the prepwork for chrome is time consuming, and consequently the expensive part of the process.

Chrome is applied using a process called Electroplating. During the process electrical current flowing from an anode carries dissolved metal in a solution where it is applied to the surface of cathode, or the part being plated. But while that sounds simple, in reality the plating process is complicated, requiring expensive equipment, constant monitoring of solution strengths and temperatures, not to mention strict adherence to a long list of safety and health standards. Sherm's is a zero-discharge facility, which means they have invested in, among other things, an ion exchange unit that continuously circulates and purifies process water, making it cleaner than what comes out of the tap.

When parts come into Sherm's for plating they are cataloged and inspected. Previously chromed parts are stripped and all parts are mechanically and chemically cleaned. Next the visible surfaces of the part are smoothed to remove any imperfections. If necessary some filling is done—lead is normally used for cosmetic fixes while structural repairs call for welding with the base material.

With the prepwork done the next step in plating is the copper coat, which is like primer for paint. In some cases several coats of copper will be applied and smoothed to make the surface perfect. On many early cars trim parts were made from a material often called pot metal. That name came from the fact that along with zinc "just about anything was thrown in the pot," including zinc, which has a low boiling point. During the casting and subsequent cooling process, air bubbles can be trapped in pot metal parts, which leads to corrosion and blisters under the chrome plating. The only way to repair a blistered pot metal part is to strip it, clean out the pit to get rid of the corrosion, then make the surface level using solder as a filler. The problem is lead won't adhere to pot metal, so the part is given a thin coat of brass. Although solder will stick

❱ *The happy voice answering the phone belongs to Kelly Wiley. She also compiles a written inventory and makes a photographic record of every piece that comes in for plating.*

to copper, there is a compelling reason for using brass. Intricate, ornate design work is often incorporated into the surface of these cast pieces and compared to copper a much thinner coat of brass can be applied to the piece, so even the most delicate details can be preserved.

After the part to be chromed is smooth straight nickel is applied. The equivalent of the first coat of color when painting, nickel provides a shiny reflective surface—but left unprotected nickel will tarnish. To protect the nickel the final step in the plating procedure is an application of chrome; it's like the clearcoat over paint. Surprisingly, this is the least time-consuming step of all the processes, taking only a few minutes in most cases. But that doesn't mean there aren't some tricks involved. Depending on the shape of the piece being plated there may be high and low density areas—that means areas that are prominent are high density and will attract more current and consequently a thicker layer of chrome; areas such as concaves are low density and won't receive as thick of a deposit. The cure for this is experience and specialized equipment.

Along with chrome-plated components stainless steel was used for trim pieces on '40 Fords and most other early cars. Over the years it's not unusual for the trim to collect an assortment of dings and dents, but stainless is tough and it can often be saved. Much like bodywork the procedure is to use hammers and dollies to remove dents. In some cases silver solder is used to repair rips and tears, all of which is followed by sanding and buffing. Properly done most stainless repairs are impossible to detect.

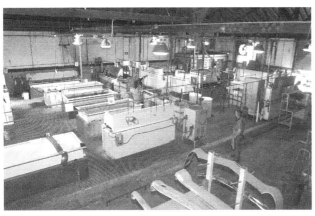

❱ Sherm's spotless facility has the most up-to-date equipment available. That's what it takes to produce quality plating and meet all applicable environmental guidelines.

❱ Art Holman demonstrates how to make chromed parts perfect. Just like paint making the surface flat makes it more reflective, copper is used as filler, and then the surface is block sanded until it all the highs and lows are eliminated.

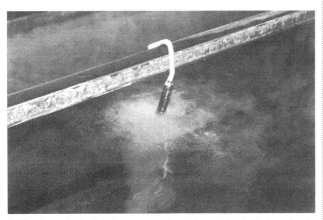

❱ All parts previously plated or not are mechanically and chemically cleaned and stripped.

❱ Every part is closely inspected during each step of the plating process. Dave Dougherty takes a close look at a bumper fresh from copper plating.

❱ Copper is the primer in the plating process. Once the copper is applied the part is thoroughly rinsed in deionized water.

❱ Once the copper-plated part is prepped it goes into the chrome tank. One of the tricks of the trade is to use a wand to direct current to low-density areas to ensure adequate material thickness.

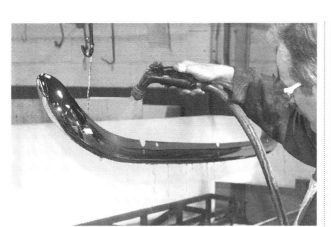

❱ Out of the chrome tank the part is rinsed thoroughly and inspected. After one more cleaning the part is inspected again and then wrapped for delivery.

❱ In this case the customer filling boltholes caused most of the damage. Never try to remove old chrome or weld up damage to save money. It will most likely cost you more in the long run.

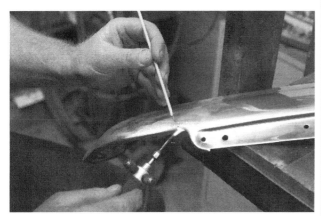

❱ It's not uncommon for stainless parts to require some repair work. In this case a crack is being repaired with flux-coated silver solder.

❱ After filling the area is sanded smooth then it's off to copper and chrome.

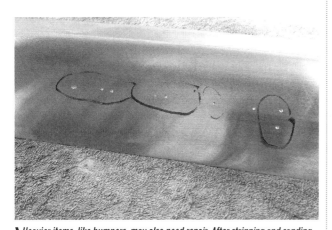

❱ Heavier items, like bumpers, may also need repair. After stripping and sanding these imperfections were obvious.

❱ During the polishing process a variety of belts, buffers, and compounds are used. The trick is to polish the surface while keeping it flat.

❱ Perfect chrome is an example of the ends justifying the means—and that means preparation is critical.

❱ Holman demonstrates the use of a sanding belt to remove some small imperfections and reveal others that will require hammer and dolly work. In any case the secret is not to get the piece too hot.

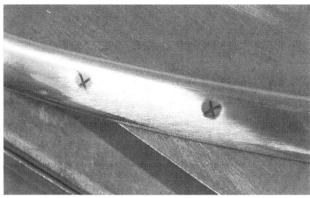

❱ Restoring stainless trim is a specialty at Sherm's. Here the dents are obvious after the surface as been lightly sanded.

❱ Once all the dents are removed the stainless is polished on a variety of wheels with an assortment of buffing compounds. The result is trim that looks better than new.

❱ Removing dents from stainless is basic bodywork. The trick is to not stretch the stainless, which is difficult, if not impossible, to repair.

❱ Resplendent in gold and chrome, the 2013 AMSOIL/STREET RODDER Road Tour '51 Ford will now sparkle in the sun.

Cooling, Plumbing, and Exhaust

✳ *BY RON CERIDONO* ✳ *PHOTOGRAPHY BY THE AUTHOR* ✳

❯ *Keeping the 2013 AMSOIL/STREET RODDER Road Tour Ford cool on the hottest of days is a radiator from Don Armstrong's U.S. Radiator.*

When the construction of any street rod is under way, including the AMSOIL/*STREET RODDER* Road Tour cars, form is usually the major consideration addressed. However, while appearance is an important factor, function must be addressed as well. And that means that the systems critical to our '51 Ford, such as cooling, plumbing, and exhaust, must operate correctly and reliably.

COOLING SYSTEM

There is nothing worse than a street rod you can't trust to keep its cool. Driving down the road with one eye on the temperature gauge is not the way to travel, neither is getting caught in traffic and watching an imitation of Old Faithful from under the hood.

Over the years we've turned to Don Armstrong at U.S. Radiator for his guidance in keeping our Road Tour car's operating temperatures in check.

Armstrong knows the radiator business; he's been at U.S. Radiator almost from the company's beginning. He began as a delivery driver, worked in every phase of radiator construction, and today owns the company. Under Armstrong's leadership the company produces radiators for over 400 different applications, and if they don't have what you need they can probably make it. To top it off, Armstrong is an avid hot rodder, so when he talks about keeping one cool, we listen. Here's what he had to say on this very important subject:

While all radiator cores might look the same, they perform vastly different based on tube spacing and fins per inch.

The heat transfer points of a radiator are where temperature is actually allowed to leave the radiator and that occurs where the fins are bonded to the tubes. The more transfer points a radiator has the greater the temperature drop will be between the inlet and outlet. For comparison, a '60s-style core typically had tubes spaced 1/2 inch apart, that is 1/2 inch of fin between the tubes. By going from a two-row radiator to a four-row core design we were able to double the heat transfer points, which resulted in a 15-20 percent increase in temperature drop without changing the other variables, such as air or coolant flow. U.S. Radiator offers four distinct core designs, the Standard that is found in most OEM-style radiators, the High Efficiency aluminum with 20 percent more heat transfer points, the High Efficiency copper/brass with 20 percent more heat transfer points, and the Optima copper/brass that uses 1/4-inch tube spacing with 1/4-inch fins that provide 40 percent more heat transfer points

Radiator materials have created quite a bit of controversy. In the '80s the Japanese came out with a core design in response to the need to downsize radiators that has become the standard in the industry because it was efficient enough to allow the re-introduction of aluminum (a less-efficient heat transfer material) at the OE level. By changing the tube spacing to 3/8 inch, a core design referred to as High Efficiency in the industry, more tubes or water passages and fins were allowed across the face of a core with a specific width in inches. The design was simple enough but proved to be very efficient in that more heat transfer points created greater temperature drop inlet to outlet. It should be pointed out that the move to aluminum radiator

construction was purely financial. The pound purchases the raw materials necessary to build a radiator and a finished aluminum radiator weighs about 25 percent of a copper/brass unit (dollars per pound being almost equal at that time). The result was a huge financial savings for the car companies.

When it comes to the difference in performance between copper/brass and aluminum radiators you may find the tests by U.S. Radiator surprising. They found that temperature drops at all operating ranges were virtually the same, with a slight advantage going to the copper/brass unit. But consider this; the thermal conductivity or heat transfer rate of copper is 92 percent versus aluminum at 49 percent. However, the copper fin is bonded to the tubes or water passages using lead solder, which is very inefficient and slows the heat transfer rate to just slightly better than that of aluminum. This can be a disadvantage if the bonding process does not allow the copper fin to touch the brass tube and why not all copper/brass cores of similar design but different manufacturers transfer heat equally. Copper/brass radiators because of their weight and durability have been around a long time and are easily disassembled and reassembled for cleaning purposes. Not the case with aluminum unless speaking of the OE version that comes with crimp-mounted plastic tanks. As a result the life expectancy of the aftermarket, aluminum radiators will be far less than that of copper/brass.

THE TRIPLE-FLOW OPTION

In most radiators coolant flows from one end of the core to the other, so it stands to reason that the longer core is the more exposure the coolant has to airflow, which would result in better cooling. Basically that's the reason crossflow radiators were developed. As cars became lower, the

only way to provide adequate core length was to make radiators shorter and wider and run the coolant side-to-side.

Of course the problem with street rods is that the length of the core is restricted by the space available. To address that issue U.S. Radiator developed the Triple Pass radiator. This unique design uses a series of baffles to re-route the coolant through the radiator core three times. As a result the coolant travels further through the core and coolant temperature can be dropped 15 to 20 percent. The Triple-Flow option is available in downflow and crossflow designs.

COOLING SYSTEM FAQS
Courtesy of U.S. Radiator

Q: What are recommended engine-operating temperatures?
A: Most hobbyists aren't concerned with fuel efficiency so our recommendation would be 175 to 195 degrees. Higher operating temps will burn fuel more efficiently but the increase in operating pressure and metal distortion can easily create problems over time.

Q: Do you recommend internal or external transmission coolers?
A: External transmission coolers are preferred to keep unnecessary heat out of the radiator.

Q: How does radiator core thickness effect cooling?
A: An increase in thickness over a stock application allows for greater fin bond surface and therefore greater temperature drop. When going from a two-row to a four-row for example you double the fin bond or heat transfer points. The increase, however, isn't a one-to-one because the transfer efficiency of the trailing rows is adversely affected by the increase in air temperature from the previous rows and the decrease in air velocity caused by the increased thickness.

Q: How much pressure should the cooling system be under?

A: We all know by increasing the system pressure by 1 pound we increase the boiling point by 3 degrees so by running a 12-pound cap our water won't boil until it gets to 248 degrees, and an engine that wants to run at 248 degrees will open that cap up long before it gets that hot. To deliberately increase the operating pressure to increase cooling is redundant in my opinion and again only points out the need for more efficient heat transfer.

Keep in mind, pressures will increase in the system just after turning off the engine as the coolant absorbs existing engine heat but can't move through the radiator to dissipate it. The resulting increase in pressure pushes coolant past the cap and hence the need for a coolant recovery system. Once the coolant in the idle engine starts to cool a vacuum is created and another valve in the cap opens and prevents the radiator from collapsing a top tank but more importantly returns the coolant to the radiator so no outside atmosphere or air (contamination) enters the sealed system. Unfortunately, most aftermarket recovery tanks are smaller than the needed capacity and that varies with cubic inches and size of the engine.

Q: How is the size of a radiator determined?

A: There are formulas to determine appropriate radiator size based on engine heat output (operating Btu) and radiator heat transfer rates (also stated in Btu). They can be found in any engineering handbook but my recommendation to a hobbyist is to put in the most efficient radiator that fits the hole or intended application, up to a four-row copper/brass or two-row aluminum core. I think everyone knows by now that copper/brass units use 1/2-inch tubes while aluminum uses 1- to 1-1/4-inch tubes. That way the thermostat or lower limit control can maintain the lowest temperature you've determined best for all driving conditions.

❭ These are tubes for a copper/brass radiator; they are pre-coated with a thin layer of solder.

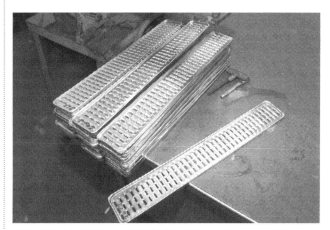

❭ Everything is built in-house at U.S. Radiator. These are the headers that are attached to the cores in copper/brass radiators. Note they accept three rows of tubes.

❭ Some radiator companies buy cores from outside suppliers; U.S. Radiator builds their own. This machine turns sheets of copper into the fins that will be placed between the tubes.

❯ Over the years U.S. radiator has accumulated the dies to reproduce a huge number of OEM radiator tanks. Of course custom tanks are routinely fabricated.

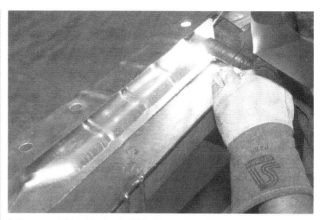

❯ Here one of the baffles for the Triple-Flow option is being welded in an aluminum tank.

❯ Tanks are stamped in-house on this press; they are made from brass or aluminum, depending on the application.

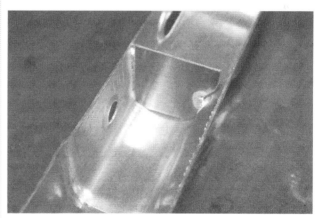

❯ This is one of the completed directional baffles in a Triple Pass radiator.

❯ Due to the volume of radiators produced, large runs of tanks are made. Here is a supply of aluminum tanks in front, with copper versions in the rear.

❯ The first step in assembling a copper/brass radiator is putting the core in a fixture and attaching the top header.

❯ Next the bottom header is installed.

❯ After the cores have cooled sufficiently the headers are dipped in solder to permanently attach the tubes.

❯ Once the headers are in place this roller is used to make sure the openings in the ends of all the tubes are uniform.

❯ Here is a header that has been soldered. Note this radiator has four rows of tubes.

❯ The core assembly is sent through an oven, which melts the solder on the tubes, securing them to the fins.

❯ These completed cores will have been matched with tanks with the proper inlet and outlet locations.

❱ These are side straps, or mounting brackets, for aluminum radiators.

❱ A Thermo-Anemometer is an evaluation tool that can be used to measure airflow or air temp.

❱ U.S. Radiator can supply custom fan shrouds for virtually any their radiators; they can be used with mechanical fans or mount an electric.

❱ Don Armstrong uses it for both to evaluate cooling systems. Here he checks the airflow of an electric fan and shroud installation.

FUEL SYSTEMS 101 FROM AEROMOTIVE

Fuel systems fall into two basic categories: static or deadhead, and dynamic or return type. Static systems typically used with carburetors essentially deliver fuel "on demand." Normally the fuel pump (mechanical or electric) will supply the carburetor's needle and seat with around 7 pounds of pressure and under normal conditions the pump will keep up with demand and maintain that pressure. As fuel is used by the engine the float drops and the needle valve opens, the resulting reduction in pressure causes the diaphragm in a mechanical pump to begin moving again, or the bypass in an electric pump to close, building the pressure back to 7 psi.

Dynamic, or return-type fuel systems can be used on carbureted systems but are most often found on fuel-injected engines. With a return-style system the pump pushes fuel at 100 percent of its capacity all the time—it also pulls 100 percent of its capacity from the fuel tank all the time and that's why pumps in a return-style system are more sensitive on the inlet side (we'll discuss that further when we get to filters). With a return-style system fuel flows through the entire system at the pressure determined by a regulator—be it 7 psi for a carburetor or 60 psi for EFI. The regulator allows fuel to "bypass" and return to the tank, then as the engine begins to use more fuel, less returns to the tank.

EFI and modern engine technology have combined to create the ultimate street-driven race car. With ordinary combinations producing from 300 hp to as much as 500 hp, the stock EFI fuel system has proven flexible. Hard-core engine combinations exceed this mark with the exotic making 1,000-plus horsepower, on "the street." Applications above 500 hp universally require a complete fuel system makeover, from fuel rails to fuel pump. A key part of any fuel system upgrade is the fuel container itself. The debate is whether to modify the stock tank or install a racing fuel cell.

There are several benefits for retaining the stock fuel tank in a high-horsepower streetcar. It has a larger capacity than most fuel cells, already has a mounting location and hardware, has provisions for filling from outside the vehicle, has a cap that both vents and seals, and is already on/in the vehicle.

The drawbacks to stock fuel tank retention are more numerous but less obvious. The stock pickup/pump assembly is restrictive, requiring complete replacement with a fabricated assembly. When using a stock tank with fabricated pickup, unless the fuel level in the tank is three-quarters full or higher, the internal well, which the stock pump draws from, is far too small and poorly supplied with fuel from the rest of the tank. Faced with the demand of a large pump, drawing through a fabricated pickup, it has no chance of refilling fast enough to support WOT full

engine load. Under low demand, cruise-type conditions, the large volume of fuel delivered to the rails is unused and returned. The same fuel, picking up heat from the pump and the rails, is constantly recycled to and from this well, rapidly increasing fuel temperature. Common problems associated with stock fuel tanks and fabricated pickups are pump cavitation, vapor lock, varying fuel pressure, exaggerated pump wear, and lean conditions during both low and high loads.

FUEL FILTERS

Filters are rated by the size of contaminates they will trap (a micron is 1/1000 of a millimeter or 0.00003937 of an inch). Aeromotive recommends that 100-micron stainless steel filter elements be used on the suction side of the fuel pump, but not all 100-micron filters are created equal. Another factor is the filtration area. Aeromotive's smaller filters have over 63 square inches of filtration media, ensuring there is ample room for flow and eliminating any pressure drop. It's not uncommon for a fuel pump to be ruined because the 100-micron fuel filter used only had 1 square inch of filtration media. The small filter area can create a huge restriction, which vaporizes the fuel causing cavitation that will lock up the pump. Common filters that cause these issues are those that use a disc-style screen. Always look at the micron rating and the filtration area. Both are equally important to the life of your fuel pump. When installing a fuel filter on the inlet of an Aeromotive fuel pump only use an Aeromotive 100-micron PN 12304, 12302, or an acceptable equivalent. On the outlet, Aeromotive recommends PN 12301 or 12310 filter with 10-micron fabric for all Aeromotive pumps except the Pro Series EFI pump, which requires filter PN 12302 with larger stainless steel element and -12 inlet and outlet fittings.

FUEL LINE FAQS

Courtesy of Aeromotive

Q: What size pump supply line should be used?

A: The size of the line from the tank to the pump's simple rule of thumb is: Do not make it smaller than the pump's inlet port size, and don't hesitate to make it bigger if you can. This is easy to figure out when the pump ports are ORB-AN type. For example, if the pump inlet port is ORB-10 use an AN-10 or larger fuel supply line, and make sure the tank or fuel cell outlet pick up tube (whatever the pump is drawing through inside the tank) is the same AN size. When you're dealing with NPT threaded ports, use the line size that is a minimum 1/8-inch larger than the NPT port thread, for example 3/8-inch NPT should have 1/4-inch (AN-08) lines, 1/2-inch NPT should have 5/8-inch (AN-10) lines. By the way, the subject of AN, NPT, and line sizes are fully addressed in Tech Bulletin PN 901 for those who want more detail.

Q: What size feed line to the engine is appropriate?

A: From the fuel pump to the engine, in low pressure (carbureted) systems use a line equal to the fuel pump outlet port for optimum results. For fuel-injected engines, the above applies, but you may use a line that is one AN size smaller than the fuel pump outlet port and still get acceptable results.

Q: What about the return line and what are the rules there?

A: In order to determine the minimum return line size you must consider the actual system pressure needed (is it carbureted or EFI?) and factor in the chosen fuel pump's output-flow. If we could, let's put one myth to bed here, there is NO "rule of thumb" relationship between the line size feeding the regulator from the pump and the line size that should be used to return from the regulator back to the tank. There are a couple of factors and one rule that can help here. Factor One: The lower the system pressure will be, the larger the return line must be (so if you're converting from EFI to carbureted, be prepared to install a larger return line, sorry!). Factor Two: The higher the fuel pump flow rate, the larger the return line must be. And The Rule: The return line size must be large enough to handle the flow from the pump while creating at least 3 psi less back pressure than the regulator is set for.

As you may have noticed, none of this has anything at all to do with the size of the supply line. The single biggest return line mistake we see, and it comes up every day, is the person who has reduced the return port in the regulator to a smaller return line. Having done this, the call comes in to report a defective regulator because they can't get the pressure to go down. What is the foolproof rule? Treat the regulator return port exactly as you do the fuel pump inlet port … You can always make the return line bigger than the regulator return port, just like you can make the suction line bigger, and contrary to what you may have heard this will have NO negative impact on pressure control. Of course, if you do make it smaller you run the risk of creating too much return restriction, resulting in a regulator that won't adjust and causing false-high fuel pressure, carburetor flooding, driveability problems, and so on. Note: When using the regulator return port size to determine the size return line to run, the same NPT to AN rules mentioned above apply.

Q: What are some general rules to follow when routing fuel lines? It's common sense to keep them away from moving parts, but what other not-so-obvious mistakes should be avoided?

A: This one's pretty easy. It's best to keep the lines secure. That can be one of the most common pitfalls made. Properly secure the lines to ensure that they do not move and incidentally rub or bump a moving part. The other side of coin would be to try and avoid heat sources wherever possible. Keeping the fuel cool is important to the system and it will pick up enough heat as is with the radiant heat from the pavement and the engine bay. Avoid placing them next to exhaust pipes.

FUEL

The original gas tank in the 2013 AMSOIL/*STREET RODDER* Road Tour '51 Ford had become a container for rust, dirt, and debris instead of fuel. Of course even if it wasn't in such sad shape, the modifications to the car and the addition of an electronically fuel-injected Ford twin-turbo EcoBoost V-6 made it impractical to use the original tank. What we needed was a new tank that fit the space available and had an in-tank fuel pump and a return to accommodate the EFI. To satisfy those requirements the crew at Honest Charley Speed Shop turned to Rock Valley for a fuel tank and Aeromotive for a pump.

Designing a custom fuel tank isn't particularly complicated; generally it has more to do with the space available than anything else. However there are some other considerations, such as capacity—1 gallon of gas measures 231 ci. Given the dimensions of our tank it should hold 16.6 gallons. Keep in mind there is often a difference between the size of the tank and the usable volume of fuel; in our case the fuel pump takes up a small about of space. Regardless of how much a tank is supposed to hold, avoid the temptation to cram as much fuel as possible into a fuel tank. Gas does expand with heat, so topping off with fuel then parking the car in the sun can result in fuel pouring out of the vent or filler cap.

Another factor in designing a fuel tank is weight; gasoline weighs approximately 6.2 pounds per gallon (depending upon temperature on temp). Topping off with 20 gallons of fuel adds roughly 124 pounds, which, depending on where the tank is mounted, can alter a car's ride and handling

To feed fuel to our high-tech Ford V-6, we chose an Aeromotive 340 Stealth fuel pump.

Aeromotive's in-tank pump has a host of advantages, among them is with the pump submerged in fuel it runs cooler, which translates into longer life and it's a whole bunch quieter to boot. Suitable for carbureted or fuel-injected applications it will support up to 700 hp with an EFI and 1,000 horses in carbureted supercharged applications.

Rock Valley has stainless steel replacement tanks for a wide variety of cars and they will also build custom tanks that can be broken down into two types, a reproduction of an original tank or a custom design. Customers can send a stock tank and straps and Rock Valley will fabricate replacements to fit in the stock location even if in width, depth (for more capacity), or a different sending unit are needed. In addition, an internal fuel pump can be added. A second option is to draw a sketch of the tank needed, or make a mockup, and have a custom tank fabricated.

❯ A Rock Valley gas tank supplies the fuel necessary to build a fire in our twin-turbocharged EcoBoost V-6. It's equipped with an internal Aeromotive fuel pump.

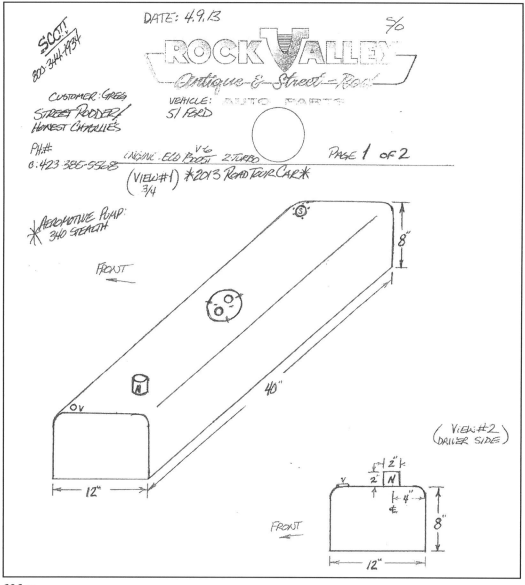

❯ We supplied Rock Valley with a sketch and they turned it into a gas tank made from 304 stainless steel; 16-gauge was used for the main body, 14-gauge for the side panels. Internal baffles were added to prevent fuel sloshing.

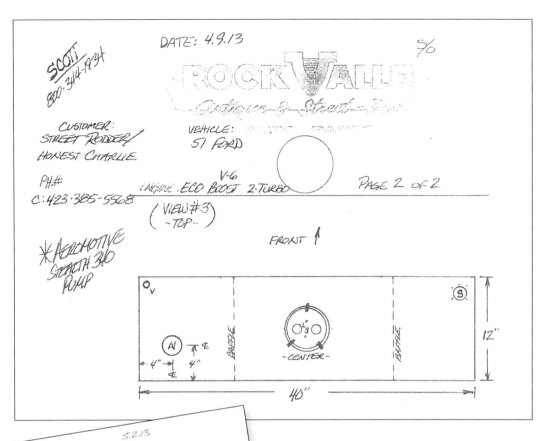

DATE: 4.9.13

SCOTT
800-344-1934

S/0

ROCK VALLEY
Antique & Street Rod

CUSTOMER:
STREET RODDER/
HONEST CHARLIE

VEHICLE:
51 FORD

PH#
C: 423·385·5568

ENGINE: ECO BOOST 2-TURBO
V-6

PAGE 2 OF 2

(VIEW #3)
-TOP-

FRONT ↑

*AEROMOTIVE
STEALTH 340
PUMP

N   ↑E   BAFFLE   -CENTER-   BAFFLE   S   V
4"   4"   12"
     ↓E

40"

S.2.13

ROCK VALLEY
Antique & Street Rod
AUTO PARTS

HELLO BRIAN—
ENCLOSED YOU'LL FIND MY DRAWINGS OF THE TANK
WE FABRICATED FOR THE 2013 "ROAD TOUR" CAR.
DETAILS OF THE TANK ARE AS FOLLOWS:

· ALL 304 GRADE STAINLESS-STEEL/NATURAL 2B FINISH
· 16GA ON MAIN BODY & 14GA. SIDE PANELS
· INTERNALLY BAFFLED
· IN-TANK PUMP SYSTEM INSTALLED w/5"DIA. SPIRAL
  SHAPED FUEL TRAP
· TIG-WELDED
· DIE-STAMPED OPENING FOR STD. 5-HOLE SENDING UNIT
  (SENDER IS AVAILABLE)
· INCLUDED A 90° ROLL-OVER CHECK VALVE FOR VENTING
· BRACKETS OF STRAPS INCLUDED FOR MOUNTING

CALL ME WITH ANY QUESTIONS OR CONCERNS YOU MAY HAVE.
THANK YOU—
SCOTT McCULLOUGH, PRES.
ROCK VALLEY ANTIQUE & STREET ROD AUTO PARTS, INC.

❱ Our Aeromotive Stealth fuel pump is mounted inside the tank. The two plugged connections are the supply line (right) and the return (left). The electrical connections are positive from a switched source (top) and ground (bottom).

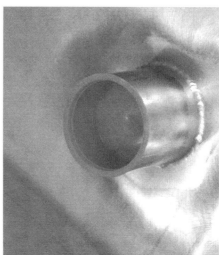

❱ Fuel fillers come in a variety of configurations. Ours accepts an extension hose, threaded, standard, and flip-up caps as options.

❱ In-tank fuel pumps have many advantages, not the least of which is the large volume of fuel keeps the pump cool, which extends its operating life. In addition, a cooler running pump won't transfer heat to the fuel, which can contribute to vapor lock. The 340 Stealth Pump provides superior flow throughout a wide pressure range. At 40 psi the 340 delivers more than 340 lph.

❱ Rock Valley installs a reinforcement plate with threaded holes to secure the fuel level sender.

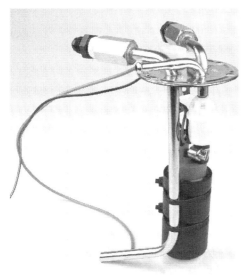

❱ A typical Aeromotive Stealth fuel pump attaches to the pickup/ return assembly and simply drops in from the top of the tank.

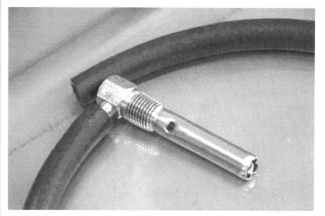

❱ As fuel is removed from the tank it has to be replaced by air so a vent is required. The type shown here has a ball-check vent valve as it prevents gas spillage but allows air to enter the tank.

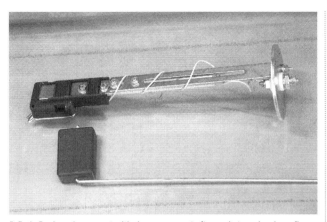

❯ Early Ford senders mount with six screws, most aftermarket senders have five. Be aware the sender and gauge used must be compatible.

❯ Filters are an important part of the fuel system. When external pumps are used Aeromotive advises to "pull through stainless, push through paper." In our case as an in-tank pump was used a paper filter was installed after the pump.

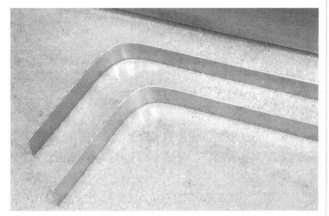

❯ Rock Valley can supply custom mounting straps or equip the tank with integral mounting tabs.

AUTOMOTIVE PLUMBING BASICS

Leaking fuel or brake lines can be catastrophic and they are often the result of improper plumbing. One of the most common mistakes made when plumbing a chassis has to do with routing—when routing brake lines, keep them away from heat sources, points of abrasion, and avoid large vertical loops, like over the rear axle, which can cause the system to trap air, and/or be difficult to bleed. Another common mistake is positioning the exhaust pipe too close to an underfloor master cylinder. It is very common for these components to be quite close, but be aware that a master cylinder, and the fluid it contains, will readily absorb heat. We've seen instances where the proximity of the master cylinder to the exhaust was such that the fluid would get hot enough to expand and make the brakes drag, or in the worst-case scenario, not release after being applied. If you opt for an underfloor master cylinder and the exhaust pipe is anywhere in the area, consider fabricating some sort of heat shield.

BRAKE LINES

A common misconception is that there is a relationship between brake line size and hydraulic pressure. Simply put, there isn't. The master cylinder establishes the pressure in a brake system; all the lines do is deliver the pressurized fluid.

Brake lines are most often 3/16 or 1/4 inch in diameter and, while there will be no pressure difference between the two, there will be a difference in the amount of fluid delivered. The bigger tubing will carry more volume, so 1/4-inch line may be preferable in some instances.

Regardless of the size, when it comes to selecting the type of rigid brake lines to use, there are only two choices: steel or stainless steel. Copper or aluminum should never be used and excessive lengths of flex line, including the braided variety, should not be used, as a spongy pedal will result.

Brake lines are connected with flared fittings, and it is important to note there are two angles that are used—37 degress for AN fittings, and 45 degrees for standard automotive fittings. Single flares with reinforcement sleeves are used on 37-degree fittings; double flares are used on 45-degree fittings.

FLEX LINES

When measuring for flex lines it is critical that suspension travel and wheel movement are taken into consideration. The front wheels must be able to turn lock-to-lock and both must be able to go through full suspension compression and rebound without putting stress on the hoses. More than one builder has jacked their car up only to yank the brake hoses apart because they weren't long enough with the suspension fully extended.

❯ To make the proper double flare on our custom brake lines we used an Eastwood kit.

❯ A second die is used to make the second portion of the double flare.

❯ These dies are used to form the first of a double flare.

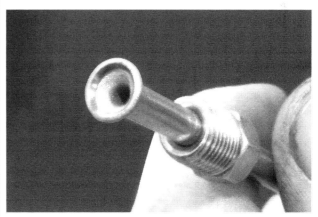

❯ A perfect double flare—it will provide a safe, leak-free connection.

❯ With the steel line clamped in the die, hydraulic pressure is used to form the first flare.

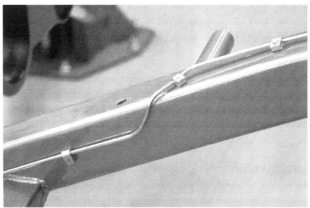

❯ Creating brake lines is part mechanical ability and part art. Lines have to be bent to fit tightly to the frame while fitting in around various obstacles.

EXHAUST

Every street rodder knows an exhaust system has to be leak-free to prevent deadly carbon monoxide from accumulating in the passenger compartment. Every street rodder also knows that the sound of the exhaust system is critical, and without a doubt the most recognizable sound to ever come out of a tailpipe is the result of a Flowmaster muffler.

In 1983, California Sprint Car racers were experiencing "excessive sound" issues at numerous racetracks and were told to quiet the cars down or lose racing privileges. All attempts to silence the race engines without sacrificing power repeatedly failed. Ray Flugger applied his 45-plus years of exhaust design experience, and out of an 800-square-foot barn in Kenwood, California, came Flowmaster's first patented design of racing silencers. Flugger attached handles to ease carrying the square-shaped race mufflers through the race pits, and the mufflers became known as "suitcase mufflers." These innovative mufflers were the result of years of development with top race engine builders, thousands of hours of dyno research, and "real-world" on-track testing. It wasn't long before Flowmasters found their way to the street where that very identifiable rumble was often heard.

In response to requests for components from shops and do-it-yourselfers, Flowmaster has developed a number of kits to make building a custom exhaust system easier than ever.

FLOWMASTER KITS

Outlaw Series feature race-bred components with only slight reduction on sound over open-exhaust tubing on non-catalytic converter–equipped vehicles. With new vehicles featuring catalytic converters, Outlaw Systems can be compatible with regular street driving. This system provides the ultimate in aggressive-sounding performance.

American Thunder Series has the classic sound of a Flowmaster chambered exhaust, which are tuned to deliver more power, torque, throttle response, and mileage. These exhaust systems deliver that authentic Flowmaster sound.

American Thunder Pro Series deliver that same great aggressive exhaust note as the American Thunder chamber exhaust system, but with a deeper, uniquely special tone due to the use of our laminar flow muffler technology.

DBX series features Flowmaster's newest laminar flow technology muffler. The DBX delivers the same attributes as the American Thunder Pro Series mufflers with a deep tone and great overall acceleration sound, but in a compact case perfect for smaller vehicles. The DBX features 304 stainless steel casings so they can be polished.

Force II Exhaust System perfect for those looking for increased performance and tone enhancement, but are concerned about installing an exhaust system that is too aggressive for daily street driving. The Force II exhaust systems commonly incorporate larger displacement mufflers and resonators to control overall sound, but increase the "performance impression" made by the vehicle.

MANDREL BENDS

All Flowmaster kits are manufactured with mandrel-bent tubing for smooth high-flow bends, which are not only aesthetically pleasing but speeds the exit of waste exhaust gases unlike compression-bent tubing found from other manufacturers or muffler shops. A typical compression-bent tubing exhaust system can easily limit exhaust gas flow by 40 percent, which not only robs your engine of torque and horsepower but also wastes fuel and creates unwanted tuning resonances in the exhaust system.

BALANCE PIPES, H-PIPES, X-PIPES

An H-pipe, commonly referred to as an equalizer, balance, or crossover pipe, connects the two exhaust pipes. It will balance the pressure of the exhaust pulses in the system, thereby reducing interior and exterior sound while increasing power. In general, the H-pipe should be installed as close as possible to the header collector. With manifolds, the H-pipe is placed just past where the downpipes become horizontal. H-pipes should be the same diameter as the main pipes or no more than 1/2-inch smaller. Flowmaster also offers a Universal Scavenger crossover pipe that is a great application in any high-horsepower racing applications. It uses D-Port Tuning technology, which helps with scavenging of waste exhaust gas and builds torque.

TAILPIPES

Tailpipes aide in keeping atmospheric pressure from rushing back into the muffler. Tailpipes can improve performance and control sound. In addition, tailpipe length can affect the power as well as sound. Tailpipes should be a minimum of 10 inches, and not longer than 6 feet. Tailpipe length of more than 6 feet may need a resonator.

POSITIONING OF MUFFLERS

The preferred location of the muffler is midway in the system, 18 inches back from the header collector. Other reasons to put them there is for improved interior resonance and sound control.

HEAT CONTROL AND SHIELDING

Heat shielding may be needed where exhaust pipes pass close by electrical, fuel, or brake lines as temperatures in

❯ Due to the twin-turbo arrangement, the stock Ford EcoBoost exhaust manifolds were retained.

❯ For leak-free joints, and to make the system easy to install and remove if necessary, the Flowmaster exhaust system uses ball and socket connectors.

❯ The Honest Charley Garage crew fabricated the exhaust system with components in a U-Fit Dual exhaust kit from Flowmaster, PN 815937. The H-pipe is also available in kit form.

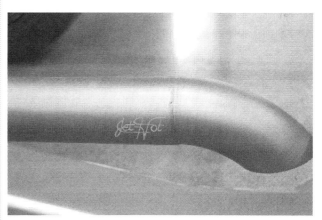

❯ To provide a long-lasting finish that not only looks good but prevents corrosion, the entire exhaust system was coated by Jet-Hot.

❯ Flowmaster DBX mufflers with 3-inch inlets and outlets were installed, PN 13014310.

❯ The 3-inch pipes snake their way thorough the crossmembers, up and over the rearend and turn down in front of the rear bumper. Note the rubber-insulated hangers that allow some movement while preventing rattles.

the exhaust system can exceed 1,200 degrees. For heat control, Flowmaster offers both tailpipe and muffler head shields.

SUGGESTED PIPE SIZES

The size of pipe used in an exhaust system is a critical item to consider. Pipe diameter will affect the sound level and performance characteristics of the muffler, but keep in mind that bigger is not always better. Too large of a pipe can actually hinder exhaust scavenging by allowing atmospheric pressure to move back up the pipe. As a rule, most street applications use 2.00- to 2.50-inch pipe, while modified street applications will generally use 2.50- or 3.00-inch.

MUFFLERS

Super 10 Series Delta Flow: Flowmaster's new Super 10 series mufflers are so aggressive that they are not recommended for use on street-driven vehicles. Best suited to racing applications, they utilize the same patented Delta Flow performance technology used in Super 40 and Super 44 series mufflers and are constructed with durable 409S stainless steel for long life and are offered in a variety of inlet/outlet configurations.

Super 44 delivers a powerful rich tone and is the most aggressive, deepest sounding, highest performing 4-inch case street muffler Flowmaster offers. Available in either 4095 stainless steel with a lifetime warranty or 16-gauge aluminized steel with a 3-year warranty, these mufflers feature Flowmaster's Delta Flow Technology design and are fully MIG-welded for maximum durability.

Flowmaster Original Series 40 is the muffler that started it all. It provides that aggressive "Flowmaster Sound" from both inside and out of the vehicle.

Super 40 utilizing Delta Flow Technology, this muffler gives the best performance to higher-horsepower vehicles. The Super 40 features a black, oversize case, which keeps the resonance down while the deep outside tone says it's a Flowmaster!

Flowmaster 40 Series Delta Flow the two-chamber design incorporates Flowmaster's patented Delta Flow technology. The "Delta" deflectors generate increased scavenging for better performance and reduced interior sound. Perfect for vehicles where an aggressive exterior tone is desired with reduced interior tone.

80 Series Cross-Flow often used on classic Camaros and Firebirds, this muffler fits transversely behind the rear axle and in front of the fuel tank. With single or dual inlets, the 80 Series gives excellent ground clearance, aggressive tone, and dual outlets to fit muscle cars requiring this specialized fitment. Constructed of 16-gauge aluminized steel and fully MIG-welded for maximum durability.

The 50 Series HD Heavy Duty was designed for late-model trucks used in the most extreme working conditions. With 4-inch internal components and large case size, these mufflers help to significantly increase mileage, torque, and horsepower while greatly improving towing power acceleration. The 50 Series Heavy Duty is great for all gas and diesel applications, and they are constructed of 16-gauge steel and fully MIG-welded for maximum durability. Stainless models carry a limited lifetime warranty.

Horsepower-2 Performance is built from either 409S or 304 stainless steel; this muffler can be polished or coated for a great-looking, show-ready finish. The Horsepower-2 muffler is designed for use with street rods, customs, lowriders, and sport trucks or industrial applications where heat control and space are an issue. The Horsepower-2 mufflers feature an innovative "Cool Shell" casting, a key feature in contributing to the muffler's sound and heat control design. Advanced "flow" technology produces broadband sound cancellation for rich '50s tone.

Pro Series these round-cased mufflers deliver ground-breaking sound control while delivering maximum power and exhaust system efficiency. The fullsize Pro Series mufflers sound great on gasoline or diesel truck or racing applications. The Pro Series "shorty" mufflers are a terrific choice for muscle cars and other performance vehicles where great sound is desired.

DBX series these mufflers utilize cutting-edge laminar flow technology drawn from both the Horsepower-2 and Pro Series muffler lines to provide maximum performance and deliver a sound quality like no other. The key to its superior performance and smooth refined tone is the patented core design, which delivers maximum exhaust efficiency, while at the same time minimizing the interior drone that is associated with other performance mufflers.

Flowmaster 50 Series Delta Flow are designed to reduce interior sound and resonance. This compact exterior case size muffler features a Resonance Tuning Chamber. This three-chamber muffler provides the same performance as the two-chambered Flowmaster mufflers and delivers increased engine efficiency for better power and mileage.

Flowmaster 60 Series Delta Flow will increase horsepower and torque in most four- and six-cylinder vehicles. This large case, short design mufflers have shown significant improvements in mileage. Helping to save fuel on many commuter vehicles, the mellow tone making for a pleasant and quiet driving experience. Constructed of 16-gauge aluminized steel and fully MIG-welded for maximum durability.

Super 50 (formerly called 50 SUV) incorporates an increased case size with the innovative technology found in the 50 Series Delta Flow mufflers. The Super 50 Series' large tuning chamber allows for optimum exhaust flow, increased mileage, and reduced interior resonance. This muffler is especially suited for trucks and SUVs as well as fullsized, high-performance street cars looking to reduce interior resonance and tone levels for everyday driving.

70 Series Big Block Muffler uses a longer case for increased volume and added sound reduction that will still fit many applications where the wider 50 Series Big Block muffler won't fit. The 70 Series Big Block utilizes Delta Flow Technology for maximum efficiency and minimum interior resonance street cars, most trucks, SUVs, RVs, and tow vehicles that require quiet operation with improved sound.

50 Series Big Block Mufflers are Flowmaster's largest and quietest muffler for tow vehicles, fullsize trucks, large SUVs, and RVs/motor homes. More than just compatible with big cubic inch engine application, the 50 Series Big Block incorporates a very large Resonance Tuning Chamber to almost completely reduce interior sound in large cab vehicle with enough case volume to handle engines under heavy loads—perfect for tow vehicles. Significant improvements in mileage, torque, and horsepower are to be expected from this muffler, as well as decreased engine heat and wear.

JET-HOT

The advantages of the coatings from Jet-Hot coatings are well known, and now those attributes are coupled and enhanced by a variety of new appearance options from the oldest name in the coating business. Jet-Hot now offers over 40 new premium colors and several new effects that still provide all the thermal and corrosion-protection customers have come to expect.

Jet-Hot offers a variety of coatings:

Jet-Hot Extreme 1300 series is the most popular coating among aftermarket customers. It provides exceptional heat management, prolonging the life of parts while enhancing performance. Available in classic polish and multiple colors, Jet-Hot Extreme 1300 will hold its luster year after year and is covered by a lifetime warranty.

Jet-Hot Extreme 2000 is often associated with turbo applications and can withstand temperature environments of 1,300-2,000 degrees F. Jet-Hot Extreme 2000 is available in black, gray, and several other colors, and has a gritty, rough texture.

Jet-Hot Extreme 2500 series eats these for breakfast … with cayenne pepper on top. So if you need serious heat management with major corrosion protection, bookmark this page.

JET-HOT MAINTENANCE TIPS

When dyno testing or breaking in a new motor or valvetrain it is very important to ensure adequate cooling of heat-quenched coated exhaust components. Stagnant air or no vehicle movement combined with high-rpm settings can result in component temperatures exceeding the limitations of the aluminum in the coating matrix. To eliminate this problem, we suggest a large fan be used to dissipate and transfer heat.

To maintain a beautiful finish and prevent corrosion for years to come, periodic maintenance of the coating is required. We recommend periodic cleaning of your parts to remove road grime, salt, and oil from the coatings, and any non-abrasive aluminum polish for heavily oxidized or stained coatings.

Stains such as oils, transmission fluid, and antifreeze can be easily removed with fine steel wool or Scotch-Brite (red) and any non-abrasive aluminum polish. After removing the stains, polish to a high luster with the aluminum polish and a soft cloth.

Colors other than polished aluminum require special handling when installing. These are all top-coated systems and the pigments can be very soft in nature. Although tougher than paints, they should be handled with the same care. Remember, all of Jet-Hot's top-coated systems protect against corrosion and thermal fatigue.

Unequal fuel distribution or advanced spark timing can result in extreme EGTs (exhaust gas temperatures), which will exceed the temperature limitations. Make certain all cylinders are functioning properly. Static-time your engine prior to starting it up for break-in. Please call or email Jet-Hot's technical department with any questions, (800) 432-3379 or sales@jet-hot.com.

Do not use any kind of caustic solutions to clean your Jet-Hot coated components. A variety of chemicals are being used on racetracks and highways today, so make it a habit to occasionally wash off your headers.

Comforts for the Road Tour

✳ *BY RON CERIDONO AND GERRY BURGER* ✳ *PHOTOGRAPHY BY THE AUTHORS* ✳

❯ *The interior of the 2013 AMSOIL/STREET RODDER Road Tour '51 Ford is spectacular. Honest Charley Garage (HCG) modified the stock dash and equipped it with Dakota Digital instruments and custom rally clock. The steering column is from Flaming River, the pedals and shifter are Lokar, and the seats are from Wise Guys with upholstery by HCG.*

Back when shoebox Fords were rolling off the assembly lines the electrical systems were simple. A 35-amp generator kept the 6V battery charged, not a particularly difficult task, as the list of electrical accessories was short. A radio, heater, and a clock were about the only items that required juice, unless the buyer opted to add a spot or foglights. In short, the electrical demands then were far different than they are now.

Today a long list of electron-eating devices have become common on street rods like our AMSOIL/*STREET RODDER* Road Tour cars—heat and air conditioning, power everything, elaborate sound systems, and vastly improved lighting are all part of the package.

Along with the increased demand on the electrical another concern is the need for voltage to be precisely maintained to protect the computers and other solid-state devices onboard. For those reasons, plus reliability and ease of installation, we turned to Painless Performance Products for a harness.

Installing a Painless Performance harness can be broken down into four simple steps:
1. Mount the fuse block
2. Route the wires
3. Cut off the excess wire
4. Terminate the wires

To make installation easier the wires coming from the fuse block are broken up into three groups:

Engine/Headlight: Includes high beam, low beam, park, right turn, left turn, electric fan, horn,

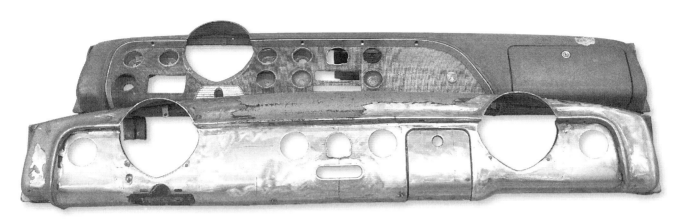

❯ HCG located a second dashboard, it was cut up to provide pieces for the modification. The "eyebrow" from a donor dash was grafted onto the right side of the original to house the clock.

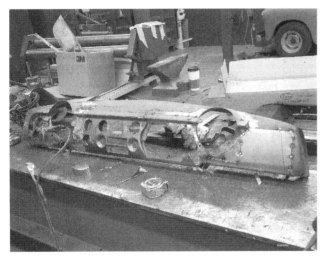

❯ The speedometer brow and the associated raised feature line were cut off the donor dashboard to be relocated on the passenger side of the dashboard. This second brow will hold a large rally clock specially built by Dakota Digital for the car.

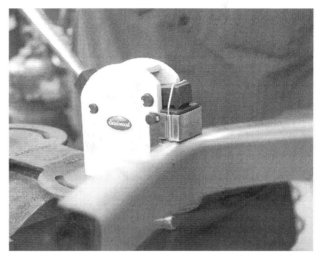

❯ Eastwood's shrinker and stretcher were put to good use, forming the additional portions of the clock "eyebrow."

starter solenoid and battery feed, alternator and alternator exciter wire, distributor, water temperature, oil pressure, and air conditioning.

Dash: Includes wires to connect gauges, indicator lights, and switches to their proper sources. Trunk accessory, door locks, power windows, and electric fuel pump are included in the 18-circuit kit.

Rear Light: Includes taillights, dome lights, left and right turn signals, brake lights, and fuel sender.

The various groups are routed to the areas where they will connect and secured to prevent damage. In some cases a wire may not be used. For instance, if the harness has a wire for an electric fuel pump and it's not used, it can be left in the harness in case a change is made at a later date. Thanks to color coding and labeling, any unused wires will be easy to identify if and when it is needed.

Painless offers a variety of kits and components to make wiring easy. The proper fuses have been pre-installed in the fuse block; all wires are color-coded and labeled. In addition, Painless kits have "accessory" terminals at the front of the fuse block that are un-fused but may be constantly hot or "switched" hot but by adding an inline fuse or circuit breaker. For safety and reliability all wire is 600 V, 125 degrees C, TXL. Standard automotive wire is GPT, 300 V, 80 degrees C, with PVC insulation.

A Look at Electrical System Components and a Few Tips

✳ *BY DENNIS OVERHOLSER, PAINLESS PERFORMANCE PRODUCTS* ✳

Circuit Breakers

Circuit breakers come in many different amperage capacities and are used in circuits the have high loads and voltage spikes. An electric fan circuit is a good example of a circuit that a circuit breaker should protect.

Wire Stranding

Did you know that in theory current flows around the strands of wire? This means that the more strands of wire in a wire the more current that wire can carry. When doing wiring of a circuit, be sure the wire is high quality and has maximum strands.

Ignition Switches

Most aftermarket ignition switches are limited to about 60 amps of current-carrying capacity. Always use caution when using a universal switch that it is not overloaded by it powering the electric fan circuit or the air conditioning circuit without a relay.

LED Flashers

LED flashers are required in many vehicles because of the installation of LED tail and front turn signal assemblies. LEDs do not pull enough current to trip the bi-metallic strip in a conventional flasher like the 1,187 styles of bulbs. LED flashers have built-in resistance to solve the problem.

Good Grounds

Grounding of your ride is essential. Always connect the battery ground to the engine and tie the engine to the frame as well as the body with heavy ground straps or cable. If your dash gauges fluctuate when you turn on the lights, there is a grounding problem.

Computers and Welding

Never weld on the chassis or other parts of your ride without disconnecting the battery and also the computer, if so equipped. Electrical surges from welding can cause internal circuitry failure in a computer and could cause gases from the battery to explode.

Alternator Output

When choosing an alternator for your ride, always ask what the output is at idle. We all idle around the fairground and the output at idle is more important than the maximum output rating. Be sure to only purchase one that has a minimum of 70 amps at idle.

Harness Routing

When installing a chassis harness and a fuel-injection harness, never route them through the same firewall hole. The radio frequency noise from the chassis harness could cause the signals from the sensors to the computer to get distorted and cause rough engine operation.

Battery Charging

When recharging the battery in your ride with a battery charger, always hook up the positive lead first to the battery and the negative lead to a good ground on the engine or chassis. This will prevent a spark close to the battery, which could cause an explosion of the batter gases.

Test Light/Voltmeter

When testing circuits, a test light or voltmeter can be used to check circuits in the main chassis harness but only a voltmeter should be used when testing circuits in the fuel-injection system. This will prevent unexpected loads on sensitive circuitry in the computer.

Electric Fans

On average, an electric fan will require 1 amp per inch of overall diameter to operate at normal speed. For instance a 12-inch fan will require 12 amps to operate but also note that twice the amperage is required during initial start-up. Be sure the circuit protection can handle the start-up load as well as the fan relay.

Hot/No Start Problems

GM large starters are well known to not activate when they get hot from driving. This is due to the solenoid plunger expanding due to the heat and sticking in its housing. A relay between the solenoid activation terminal and the battery source, to flow more current, will almost always remedy the problem.

Soldering versus Crimping

As the old saying goes "soldering is great on TV sets." Controversy is long standing on this subject. The general rule of thumb is that if you are proficient in soldering and the wires being soldered will never move, solder them. In automobiles, wires are mostly moving and vibrating, which can cause a solder joint to break the wire next to the joint. Crimping is preferred.

SOLID-STATE DEVICES

The term solid state means that an electrical device has no moving parts other than electrons. Some of the common solid-state devices found in trucks are:

Diodes: These are one-way electrical valves; current can flow one way but not the other. Diodes are found in a number of places, most notably in alternators. They help transform alternating current to direct current.

Light-Emitting Diodes: Becoming more common all the time, LEDs have a small lens built in. The flow of electrons generates energy released in the form of light. Unlike a conventional bulb, no heat is created.

Transistors: These are solid-state switches used in applications like electronic ignitions to turn a circuit on and off, or in a stereo to strengthen a radio signal.

Resistors: Used to limit current flow, resistors can have a fixed value or they can be adjustable (also called a potentiometer).

Capacitors: A capacitor can store an electric charge. The condenser in a point-style ignition is actually a capacitor. Some electronic ignition systems use a capacitor to store an electrical charge that is released all at once.

GAUGES

The original gauges found in most cars of our Ford's era are less than accurate—rather than supplying specific information they provide little more than a rough idea of what's going on in the systems they were meant to monitor.

To provide the kind of feedback we deemed necessary we turned to Dakota Digital for a unique gauge and clock package for our '51.

As the name implies, Dakota Digital has specialized in digital instrumentation and they are based on the outskirts of Sioux Falls, South Dakota. And while they built their reputation by offering an amazing array of high-tech digital gauges they also offer a complete line of analog gauges. These new VHX instruments feature a state-of-the-art stepper motor that moves the needle a precise number of degrees based on electrical input from the sender. A microprocessor updates input to the motor and the needle deflects accordingly. The VHX gauges have fully lit needles, backlit faces, and highly visible LCD message centers.

Displays included with the VHX system:

Speedometer: 0-120/140/160 mph analog, depending upon application, 0-255 mph/kph digitally in message center.

Tachometer: 0-8,000 analog, 0-9,990 digitally in message center.

Oil Pressure: 0-80 psi analog and digitally.

Water Temp: 140-220 degrees F analog, 0-300 degrees F/0-150 degrees C digitally in message center.

Voltmeter: 0-17 VDC analog and digitally.

Fuel Level: Empty-Full analog, 0-99 percent digitally in message center.

Also shown in the digital message center: odometer, trip odometer (A&B), resettable service odometer, clock, hour-meter, 0-60 mph (0-100 kph) timer, quarter-mile timer, quarter-mile speed display, high-speed recall, and high-rpm recall.

Various indicators can also be displayed such as: turn signals, high beam, check engine, parking brake, and cruise control.

Automatic Transmission gear indicator is also included, which will display the full name (park, overdrive, and so on) of the current gear. Utilizing the gear position indicator will require the use of a Dakota Digital GSS-2000 sending unit (sold separately).

Dakota Digital instrument systems also include a demonstration mode, which will cycle the instrument readouts while the vehicle is standing still. This is especially popular while the vehicle is on display at a show, event, or simply displaying the instrument system.

Metric conversions will cycle between mph and kph in the digital message center with the press of a button. Full metric analog instrument systems (kph and celsius) are not currently available.

Necessary sensors included for oil pressure (1/8-inch NPT), water temp (1/8-inch with bushings for 1/4-, 3/8-, 1/2-inch NPT, as well 12mm and 16mm for GM and LS applications), and speedometer pulse generator.

Fuel level gauge can read either OEM sensor, or any aftermarket style currently available. A universal fuel level sender (PN SEN-06-1) can be purchased from Dakota Digital if necessary.

Fully programmable speedometer for various tire sizes, rearend gearing combinations, and so on.

Built-in illumination is activated as headlights/parking lights are activated. The DIM-1 can be purchased from Dakota Digital to increase or decrease the brightness of the display. The DIM-1 is used in conjunction with your headlight switch.

Fully adjustable warning points alert the user of potential vehicle problems in the digital message center.

If that's not enough information, an assortment of specialty displays can be added as well, such as boost, trans/oil temps, compass, air ride system pressures, and inside/outside temps.

Dakota Digital installed all the speedometer, tach, volt, gas, water temperature, and oil pressure gauges in an original '51-style housing. Also included in our array of instruments are two clocks. In the center of the dash is a digital clock that not only keeps time accurately but also with the push of the appropriate button will display the same information center data that is contained in the main instrument pod. In addition, a custom, battery-powered rally clock, like those used in the Honest Charley Garage (HCG) and Coker-sponsored Great Race, can be found in the dash on the passenger side.

POWER WINDOWS

Thanks to Specialty Power Windows (SPW), raising and lowering the door the movement of a stock-appearing window crank actuated switch does glass electrically.

SPW is unique in that they are devoted exclusively to the manufacture of power window kits, windshield wiper kits, and related pieces that are manufactured in their facility, they are not simply "repackaging" components from other suppliers.

The SPW universal street rod kit we installed uses GM motor and cable lift drives and GM switches. It came complete with a wire harness with switch and motor plugs, a flexible stainless steel wire conduit kit for the door openings, and lower glass channels. The regulator only requires 8-1/2 inches of clearance beneath the glass and bottom of door. Simple to install, this lift kit completely replaces the original regulators and crank handles.

ELECTRIC WIPERS

For the truly effective windshield wipers that are a necessity on any street rod that is driven, SPW offers their flex shaft system. This universal Dual-Wiper Drive Kit has two wiper shafts that will accept arms that fit 1/2-inch fine spline knurls or arms that fit 1/4-inch shafts. The output shafts are driven by a remote-mounted, commercial duty, two-speed wiper motor with 300 in/lb stall torque. The sweep is adjustable from 90 to 160 degrees in 10-degree increments.

SPW Dual-Wiper Kits are available with two-speed intermittent self-park switch kits or two-speed self-park switch kits. Two-speed switch kits are available with either a rotary knob or black rocker switch. SPW advises that dual wiper kits are best suited for cars under construction, as some applications will require modifications to the original holes. All universal kits come with written and video instructions. Standard kits come with a 72-inch drive cable with 144-inch drive cable and tubing as an option.

HEAT AND A/C

To provide climate control in our Road Tour Ford we again turned to Vintage Air. Jack Chisenhall opened the doors to Vintage Air in 1976, initially installing air-conditioning systems in late-model vehicles and trucks. As the business grew kits for street rods and muscle cars were developed. Vintage Air has worked with several OEM companies to meet their needs for performance climate-control systems. A diehard hot rodder, in 1995 Chisenhall ran 241 mph at Bonneville in his '53 Studebaker with the air conditioning on to demonstrate the reliability and performance of Vintage Air's systems.

Vintage Air has always taken a "complete system" approach to their product line, and that's what HCG installed in our Road Tour '51—a complete Gen IV Magnum Universal fit system.

The Gen IV is Vintage Air's most powerful and refined climate-control system and has the following features:
- Electronic controls without cable or vacuum actuators
- Microprocessor-controlled coil temperature monitor, no capillary tube to install
- Separate high-capacity heat and cool coils
- Aluminum plate/fin A/C coil (most efficient evaporator design available)
- Copper/brass parallel flow heater coil
- Blend air door for instant temperature adjustment
- Infinite dash/floor air blend (in most applications)
- Infinite defrost/floor air blend with dedicated defrost option
- All Gen IV systems allow for optional smooth firewall configuration (must use modified hose kit)
- Positive shut-off solenoid operated heater control valve in max A/C

The heating system in our Vintage Air unit is much more sophisticated than Ford's original heater. First and foremost the volume of heat delivered is far greater; temperature control is much more precise and the defrosters are extremely effective. Contemporary electronic heater valves shut off the flow of hot water when heat is not needed, or wanted.

Cooling the air is a little more complicated than heating it. In simple terms air conditioners make the air cold by removing heat—here's how the experts at Vintage Air explain the parts and operation: The components of an automotive air conditioning system are the compressor, compressor bracket, evaporator (inside car unit), condenser (outside heat exchanger), hoses and fittings, the drier, and a safety switch.

Now, here's how they operate: The compressor pumps refrigerant, in gas form, into the high-pressure gas discharge line. This gas is loaded with heat it has absorbed from the air flowing over the evaporator coil inside the vehicle.

As the heated high-pressure gas reaches the condenser that is typically mounted in front of the radiator, the air flowing through it carries off the heat. The refrigerant condenses into a liquid, which pours into the receiver/drier where it falls to the bottom of the receiver. A pickup tube fits into the receiver/drier almost reaching the bottom of the tank (the open end of the tube is always below the liquid level in the receiver/drier, if the system is fully charged), which provides pure liquid to the line between the drier and the expansion valve.

The expansion valve is an orifice that varies in size according to the temperature of the evaporator coil. By changing size, it meters the refrigerant according to the demands of the evaporator. When warm, the orifice is largest and gets smaller as the evaporator gets colder. This orifice provides a pressure drop with the resulting drop in refrigerant temperature. The high-pressure liquid pours into the larger opening of the evaporator and the low-pressure liquid droplets begin to pick up heat, which expands the refrigerant to a low-pressure, super-heated gas, which then returns to the compressor to start the cycle all over again.

Basic Air Conditioning Components

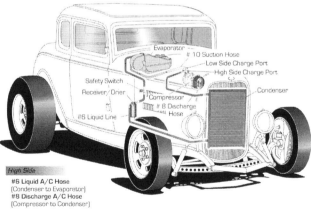

Evaporator
10 Suction Hose
Low Side Charge Port
High Side Charge Port
Safety Switch
Receiver/Drier
Compressor
Condenser
8 Discharge Hose
#6 Liquid Line

High Side
#6 Liquid A/C Hose
(Condenser to Evaporator)
#8 Discharge A/C Hose
(Compressor to Condenser)

Low Side
#10 Suction A/C Hose
(Evaporator to Compressor)

Direction of Refrigerant Flow Indicated By Arrows

Each year our AMSOIL/*STREET RODDER* Road Tour car logs roughly 25,000 but this time around we've added something new. The car is being built at HCG, a company that is part of the Coker Tire group—and when it comes to driving old cars, the Coker family loves to participate in vintage car rallies, including The Great Race. Since vintage car rallies are open to modified and original cars, the plan is to take this chopped and channeled, twin-turbo Ford-powered hot rod on a vintage car rally. To meet the needs of that particular activity, this car is going to be equipped with a rally clock, specially designed by Dakota Digital, that will allow the navigator to accurately time the prescribed routes. That means the '51 Ford dashboard must be modified to accept this rather large timepiece.

The '51 Ford dashboard is no doubt the best-looking dash of all the '49-51 shoebox Fords. None of this was lost on Greg Cunningham and the team at HCG, so they carefully planned a dashboard modification that would still carry the great '51 Ford look, but also provide room for the aforementioned clock and new Dakota Digital instruments.

To accomplish this task a second '51 Ford dashboard donated the speedometer "brow" and some of the raised portion of the dashboard. Then Richard Marter deftly cut up the pieces and welded them to the original dash. The original glovebox was sacrificed, but the glovebox door was sectioned and relocated toward the center of the dashboard. Vintage Air in-dash outlets were located and then the dash was ready for final prep and paint. When it was all completed it looked like a dashboard that could have been stamped in Dearborn in 1951.

With the dashboard remodeled, the HCG crew turned their attention to finishing the remainder of the interior. One of the major tasks was dealing with the 6R-80 SelectShift automatic transmission. While transmissions aren't normally a factor when designing an interior, the Ford six-speed requires a huge tunnel in the floor so the decision was made to build a center console. Not only does the centerpiece accommodate the transmission's intrusion into the passenger compartment, it provides storage space and it looks cool. To further the cause of comfort, all the interior surfaces were covered in Dynamat, Specialty Power Windows were installed along with new rubber seals from SoffSeal.

Although our '51 was originally equipped with a rear bench seat, we elected to make it into the Road Tour version of a business coupe to accommodate all the stuff the car carries on the road. Up front a pair of Wise Guys buckets were covered in a combination of black vinyl and N.O.S. black and gray '58 Buick cloth. All the stitchwork was done in house at HCG.

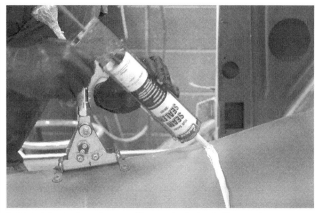

❯ All the joints in the replacement floor received a bead of Eastwood seam sealer to eliminate the possibility of water or fumes entering the passenger compartment.

❯ By combining and reshaping parts of the raised feature line from the donor dash Richard Marter was able to get a perfect fit on the end of the dashboard. The very bottom of this piece was tapered to an end and once the piece was fitted a line was drawn on the dash by following the edges of the new piece.

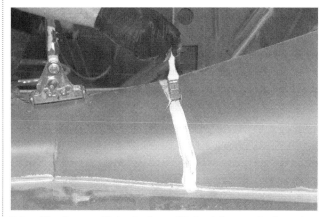

❯ A small brush was used to level and spread the bead of seam sealer. Once set, the sealer can be primed, painted, or left as is.

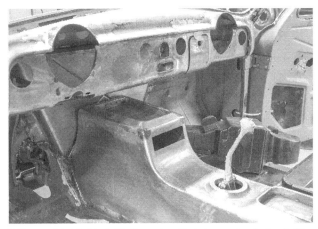

❯ The remodeled dash looks like it came from the factory, as does the handbuilt console built to accommodate the six-speed automatic and house the stereo and Lokar shifter.

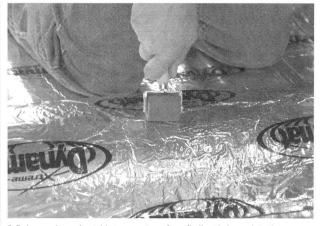

❯ To keep noise and outside temperatures from finding their way into the passenger compartment the entire interior was treated to products from Dynamat.

❯ Installing Dynamat requires only a few tools: rags and a solvent-based cleaner (rubbing alcohol also works) to prepare the surface, a razor knife or scissors for trimming, and a roller tool to press the self-adhesive material in place.

❯ The Painless fuse panel and a variety of relays were cleverly hidden behind the right rear upholstery panel. Still easily accessible, there's no clutter under the dash.

❯ Contained in one housing are the Dakota Digital VHX instruments—speedometer, tach, fuel, oil, temp, and volt gauges along with a digital information center (note the plastic protecting the lens is still in place).

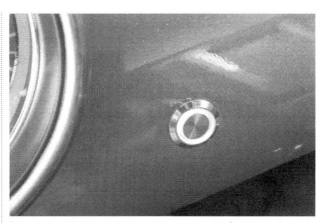

❯ The EcoBoost V-6 is controlled by a Painless push to start/push to stop button in the remodeled dash.

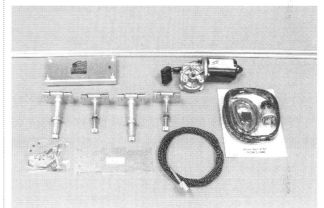

❯ Keeping the windshield clear during inclement weather are wipers from Specialty Power Windows (SPW).

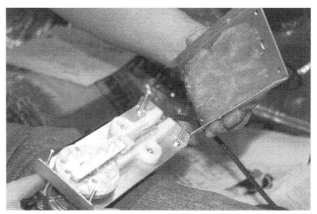

❯ The SPW windshield wiper motor spins a wheel that in turn pushes and pulls a cable to operate the windshield wipers. The arc of the wipers can be adjusted by changing the cable's attachment point on the wheel.

❯ As the cable moves back and forth this "gear" moves the wiper arm back and forth.

❯ After assembly, the wiper drives are assembled bolt-on covers to protect the internals of the gearboxes.

❯ SPW offers a variety of chrome and billet aluminum windshield wiper arms for OEM and SPW wipers.

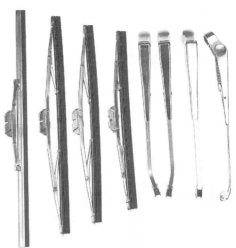

❯ Wiper blades and arms are offered for flat and curved glass in various lengths; arms are available angled and straight.

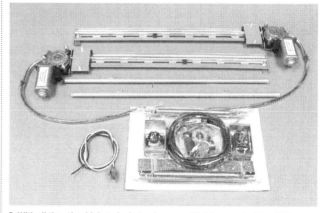

❯ With all the other high-tech electronics we couldn't be expected to roll the windows up and down manually—that chore is now handled by the push of a button, thanks to SPW.

❯ Installing the SPW universal window kit couldn't have been easier—the motor and drive assembly attaches to a plate attached to the doorframe. The plate can be bolted, riveted, or welded, as HCG chose to do.

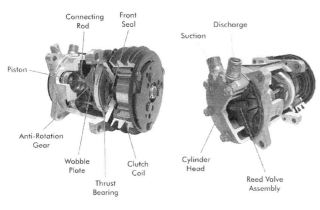

❯ The Sanden compressors used by Vintage Air are compact, smooth running, and reliable. The five connecting rods and pistons are moved by what's called a "wobble plate."

❯ This is an electronic hot water valve that eliminates cables and vacuum hoses. It must be oriented correctly—an arrow indicates the direction of water flow.

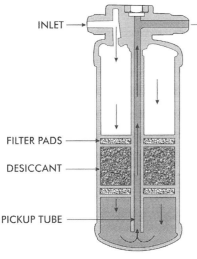

❯ This is a receiver-drier. Its functions are to separate gas and liquid and remove moisture from the system. As liquid refrigerant is picked up from the bottom of the canister, it should always be mounted vertically.

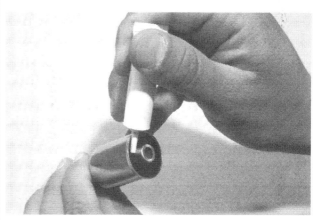

❯ A/C hoses have to be cut to length and the ends crimped on. The ends with small caps are service ports used to evacuate and charge the system. When installing ends on the hose the prescribed lubricant should be used.

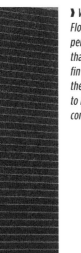

❯ Vintage Air Super Flow condensers are 40 percent more efficient than the old tube and fin design. HCG bent the solid stainless lines to make the necessary connections.

❯ The R134A systems must use barrier hose to prevent the loss of refrigerant.

❱ Because of the high pressures involved it is critical that the proper crimping tool is used for the type of ends installed.

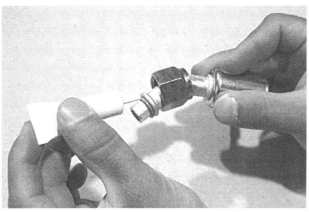

❱ The O-rings used on the fittings must be for R134A; they should be lubricated with the proper oil before installation.

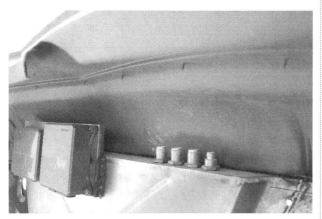

❱ To connect the A/C and heater hoses to the underdash unit, a four-port bulkhead fitting was installed in the top of the firewall recess.

❱ On the firewall side, 90-degree fittings were used to keep the hoses tucked tight to the firewall.

❱ An important part of an air-conditioning system is a safety switch. These are extremely important since an A/C system relies on refrigerant to carry lubrication through the system. This is a binary pressure safety switch; it disengages the compressor clutch in case of refrigerant loss.

❱ A trinary switch combines low-pressure protection with high system pressure protection that turns on an electric fan at 254 psi.

❯ *Vintage Air has a broad selection of dashboard outlets. It's important that none of the A/C outlets on the evaporator case are blocked off, as localized freezing of the coils can result.*

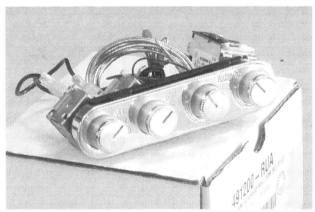

❯ *Control panels are available in a variety of configurations. We chose the Streamline version with lighted knobs.*

❯ *A Vintage Air Gen IV unit handles temperature control; it tucks close to the FAST ignition and fuel-injection control units for the EcoBoost V-6. Vintage Air offers empty mock-up evaporator cases to make placement and fabricating mounting brackets easy.*

❯ *The Vintage Air receiver/drier was mounted to the custom inner fender panels. Note the plumbing for the turbos and intercooler.*

❯ Stitching and installing the interior coverings was done in-house at HCG.

❯ HCG's head upholstery man, Greg Mills, is busy sewing up Symphony Classic vinyl.

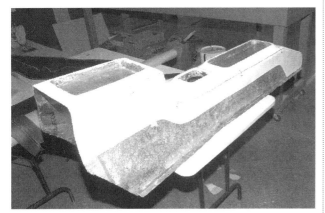

❯ Prior to upholstering, the console was covered with a thin layer of foam.

❯ From this angle the storage compartments at each end of the console can be seen; between them are the openings for the Pioneer stereo and Lokar shifter. The finished console is a combination of vinyl and carpeting. For contrast, the cover was stitched with contrasting thread.

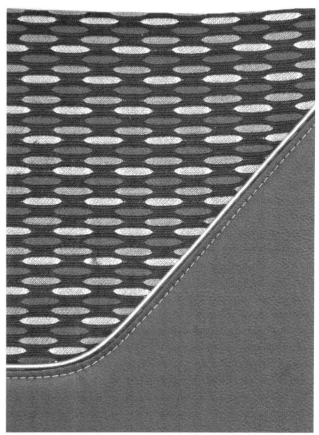

❯ The interior uses a unique combination of N.O.S. '58 Buick upholstery fabric in combination with high-quality Symphony vinyl.

❱ We've opted for Wise Guys seats in the past and have been extremely pleased with their quality and comfort. In this case we chose unupholstered buckets so they could be covered to match the rest of the interior.

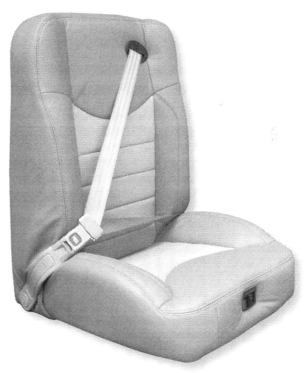

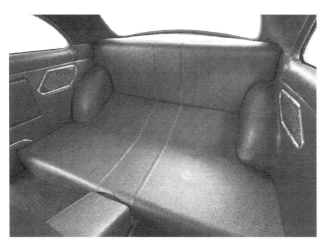

❱ In business coupe fashion, the rear seat was eliminated, however the wide-open space was upholstered with the same materials used up front.

❱ For those looking for ready-to-install seats, Wise Guys can provide bench, split-bench, buckets, and virtually any type necessary in a variety of upholstery materials.

Finishing the '51 Ford

✳ BY RON CERIDONO ✳ PHOTOS COURTESY OF THE MANUFACTURERS ✳

❱ Coker's Chattanooga showroom has a vast array of tires and wheels on display—and there's much more that can't be seen.

A Few Minutes With Corky Coker

We had the pleasure of sitting down with Corky Coker during a visit to his Chattanooga, Tennessee, facility. Anyone who is a rodder, restorer, antique motorcycle buff, military vehicle collector, unicyclist, or is somehow involved with anything vintage that has rubber wrapped around the wheels is familiar with the name Coker, arguably the best-known name in the specialty tire business.

Harold Coker had a successful BFGoodrich dealership in Chattanooga. And while the business of selling tires for everyday cars was good, as an avid antique car collector he recognized the need for specialty tires, and in 1958 the business expanded to meet that need. In 1974 his son, Corky, took over Coker Tire's antique division. Today Corky Coker runs a business he describes as an inch deep and a mile wide. It occupies 95,000 square feet of space in six buildings nestled in the historic southside district of downtown Chattanooga. In addition, there is a new wheel manufacturing plant and tire distribution center in City of Industry, California.

Coker has collected an amazing array of vehicles and he enjoys using them for their intended purpose. Telling of welding up a 1909 Lozier axle on the road and searching for an errant knock-off wheel that came off

❯ Today's showroom is a far cry from the Ford van that was used to transport virtually everything Coker offered to swap meets.

a '37 Indy car and disappeared down the road brings a smile to his face. "It's all part of the adventure," he says.

While Coker's involvement in vintage automobiles is well known, another claim to fame is his involvement in unicycling. His support has resulted in an annual 800K race in Nova Scotia and the creation of a new word—*Cokering*, a verb for unicycling.

So where's Coker going from here?

In his own words: "We're committed to the growth of the hobby," which means you can look for even a greater variety of tires to become available. Like the man says, Coker Tire is an inch deep and a mile wide, and getting wider all the time.

American Classic radial tires are made in the United States, and feature a variety of tread patterns, sizes, and whitewall widths; they feature an H-speed rating, and have an

asymmetrical tread pattern for great, all-around performance.

The tires we used on the 2013 AMSOIL/*STREET RODDER* Road Tour '51 Ford were Coker PN 6880832 American Classic Whitewall Radial, 235/55R17 with 1.75-inch whitewalls.

For those looking for options, Coker Tire offers hundreds of sizes and styles in traditional bias-ply tires and contemporary radials.

QAI PRECISION PRODUCTS

Founded in 1993, QA1 offers a variety of shock absorbers, struts, springs, suspension components, ball joints, spherical bearings, rod ends, and other related products to a variety of markets, including circle track racing, drag racing, street performance, street rodding, custom OE manufacturing, and various industrial markets. QA1 manufactures the majority of these products in their 66,000-square-foot Lakeville, Minnesota, facilities.

Tips on Selecting and Installing Coilovers:

For our application we used 550-pound springs up front and 275-pound in the rear.

To maintain the integrity of the product, it is recommended that the shock be installed at the specific ride height for each model size to protect the piston and valve assembly from possibly topping or bottoming out.

SHOCK PART #	RECOMMENDED RIDE HEIGHT	RECOMMENDED SPRING LENGTH	RECOMMENDED APPLICATION
ALN-3855	9 ¾" – 10 ¼"	7"	FRONT
ALN-4855	12" – 12 ½"	9", 10"	FRONT / REAR
ALN-5855	13 ½" – 14"	12"	REAR
DD / DS-301, 302	9 ½" – 10"	7"	FRONT
DD / DS-303, 304	10 ¾" – 11 ¼"	7", 8", 9"	FRONT
DD / DS-401, 402	11 ½ - 12 ½"	9", 10"	FRONT / REAR
DD / DS-403, 404	12 ½" – 13 ¼"	10"	FRONT / REAR
DD / DS-501, 502	13 ¼ - 14 ½"	12"	REAR
DD / DS-701, 702	15 ¼" – 15 ¾"	14"	REAR
DD / DS-801, 802	16" – 16 ¾"	14"	REAR
DD / DS-901, 902	18 ½" – 19 ½"	14"	REAR
US301, US302	9 ¾" – 10 ¼"	7"	FRONT
US303, US304	10 ¾" – 11 ¼"	7", 8", 9"	FRONT
US401, US402	11 ¾" – 12 ½"	9", 10"	FRONT / REAR
US403, US404	12 ¾" – 13 ½"	10"	FRONT / REAR
US501, US502	13 ¾" – 14 ¼"	12"	REAR
US701, US702	15 ¼" – 15 ¾"	14"	REAR

Valving Adjustment Instructions For All QA1 Adjustable Shocks

QA1 shocks have 18 damping settings per knob. There are 6 clicks per revolution of each knob, and each knob has 3 complete revolutions. The knob set fully counter clockwise is the softest setting - start your adjusting from that point. Recommended base settings to begin testing with are as follows:

Shocks with one adjuster knob:

Drag Racing: 0-6 clicks

Other Applications: 2-8 clicks for nice ride and handling; 8-12 clicks for firm ride and improved handling; 13+ clicks for more aggressive handling

Shocks with two adjuster knobs:

Drag Racing: 12-16 clicks compression and 0-4 clicks rebound

Other Applications: 2-8 clicks compression and rebound for nice ride and handling; 8-12 clicks for firm ride and improved handling; 13+ clicks for more aggressive handling

NOTE: DO NOT FORCE THE ADJUSTER KNOB. DO NOT USE PLIERS OR ANY OTHER TOOLS ON THE PISTON ROD OR THE ADJUSTER KNOB. DO NOT EXCEED 18 CLICKS UNDER ANY CIRCUM-STANCES. THIS COULD DAMAGE THE SHOCK AND CAUSE IT NOT TO ADJUST. THIS WILL VOID ALL WARRANTIES. DO NOT USE THE SHOCK ABSORBER AS A SUSPENSION/ TRAVEL LIMITER. SEVERE DAMAGE TO THE SHOCK WILL OCCUR AND DOING SO WILL VOID ALL WARRANTIES.

TECHNICAL ASSISTANCE DIAGRAMS & CHARTS

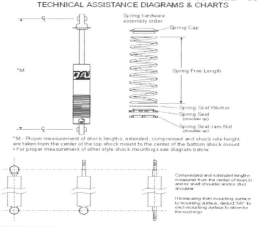

EASTWOOD

The Eastwood Company has been supplying restoration repair tools, equipment, and supplies for hobbyists and professionals alike since 1978 and they played a big part in the construction of the 2013 AMSOIL/*STREET RODDER* Road Tour '51 Ford.

Eastwood maintains an informative website that offers detailed information on their products. It includes photos, uses, prices, and customer feedback as well as a 100 percent secure shopping cart. Detailed instruction manuals are also available at eastwood.com.

Eastwood Parts List:

PN 28160	Louver Dies for Bead Roller	PN 19016	Intergrip Panel Clamps
PN 28187	Bead Roller Kit, with Mandrels	PN 11167	EW Body Solder Kit, deluxe with DVD
PN 28060 PA	Bead Roller Guide, Fence adjustable	PN 11164	*Leadwork and Plastic Filler* DVD
PN 14042	Eastwood Versa Bend Sheetmetal Brake	PN 31126 A	Eastwood Body Solder Kit Deluxe
PN 12117	Eastwood Thermocoustic Barrier	PN 31031	Flat File Holder, Adjustable
PN 11797	Throatless Shear	PN 50553	Eastwood Body Soldering Diffuser Tip
PN 70270	Three-piece Aviation Tin Snip Set	PN 28060 P	Bead Roller Guide, Fence Adjustable
PN 70245	Aviation Tin Snips Left Cut	PN 28060 Q	Adjustable Fence Instruction Sheet
PN 70246	Aviation Tin Snips Right Cut	PN 51088	Shrinker/Stretcher Combo Set, two bodies, two jaws
PN 70247	Aviation Tin Snips Straight Cut		
PN 16070 ZP	Rust Encapsulator Black Gallon	PN 25304	Professional Brake Tubing Flaring Tool
PN 16060 Z	Rust Encapsulator Black Aerosol 15 ounce	PN 49074	Eastwood Brake Forming Tool
PN 51483 Z	EW Rust Converter, new formula, Aerosol	PN 51605	Eastwood Concours Paint Gun with three tips, plastic and metal cup
PN 13651 Z	EW Rubberized Rust Encapsulator Blk Aero 15 ounce	PN 51550 G	Eastwood Concours Paint Gun with 1.2 tip
PN 12515 Z	Internal Frame Coating 14 ounce with Spray Nozzle	PN 51552	1.4 Cap/Needle/Nozzle for Concours Gun
PN 12511 Z	Internal Frame Coating 14 ounce can	PN 51553	1.8 Cap/Needle/Nozzle for Concours Gun
PN 12512	Aerosol Nozzle with 24-inch Extension Hose	PN 51550 B	600cc Aluminum Cup for 51550
PN 12846 Z	Aerosol Injected Cleaner 11 ounce Net	PN 51136	Eastwood Branded Color Paint Chart
PN 70232	Screwdriver set, Eastwood 9-piece	PN 11979	Eastwood 7-piece Professional Hammer Set
PN 70231	Flexible Ratcheting Wrench Set SAE Eastwood 7-piece	PN 28030	Eastwood Panelbeater Sandbag
PN 11251	3-piece Adjustable Profile Gauges: 5-10-15 inch	PN 28123	Set of six Mallets (Round and Teardrop)
		PN 28111	Eastwood Round Mallet 2-inch diameter
PN 11190	5-inch Adjustable Profile Gauge	PN 28112	Eastwood Round Mallet 2-3/4-inch diameter
PN 11191	10-inch Adjustable Profile Gauge	PN 28113	Eastwood Round Mallet 3-1/4-inch diameter
PN 11192	15-inch Adjustable Profile Gauge		
PN 70297	Complete Mechanics Tool Set, Eastwood 150-piece	PN 28114	Eastwood Teardrop Mallet 2-inch diameter
PN 13901	MIG Spot Weld Kit	PN 28115	Eastwood Teardrop Mallet 2-1/2-inch diameter
PN 29935	Magnetic Hole Plug Welding Tool, not for gas welder	PN 28119	Eastwood Teardrop Mallet 2-3/4-inch diameter
PN 51139	Welders Helper, 3x3 Set Flat/Curve/ Angle Cop Plates		

LOKAR

Skip and Debbie Walls, of Lokar Performance Products, have been involved in the Road Tour program since its inception—every car built has been equipped with an array of their products.

Over the last 25 years, Lokar's product line has expanded and includes automatic transmission shifters, emergency brake actuators and cables, throttle and kick-down cables, throttle assemblies (including throttle-by-wire), engine and transmission dipsticks, interior accessories, and much more.

Lokar Parts List:

PN COS6AODEM	Cable-operated Shifter AOD 8-inch Mush
PN S-7061	Floor Mount Threaded Rod Assembly
PN ACA-1802	Adjustable Trans Arm 350/400/700
PN S-6946	700 Selector with Gear Plate
PN EHB-9200	Under the Dash Emergency Handbrake
PN IDH-2009	Polished Billet Aluminum Door Handle GM and Ford 1949 and Up, Pair
PN BCA-9500	90-degree Billet Aluminum Direct Fit Automatic Brake Pedal Arm with XL Oval Pad

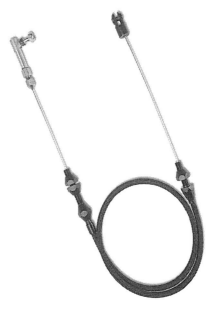

❯ Lokar's Hi-Tech throttle cables are available with stainless braided, black stainless braided, or black housings. A long list of mounting brackets and matching throttle valve cables are also available.

❯ Known for their shifters, Lokar has them for every popular automatic. A wide variety of automatic and stick shift levers are also available.

YOGI'S: THE OFFICIAL ROAD TOUR PARTS STORE

The list of parts needed to build a street rod is long, but the wait time to have those parts delivered doesn't have to be. That was the motivation behind the creation of Yogi's Inc. Yogi Sommerville knew the frustration of back-ordered and leisurely delivered parts while building his cars and he decided to do something about it.

In 1979, Yogi's sprouted in an Iowa cornfield and has since grown to be a 40,000-square-foot facility, holding 12,000 parts in stock from over 100 manufacturers. In the rare instance that they don't have a requested part, their motto is "we'll try and get it."

Thanks to Yogi's location in the heartland of the country, delivery times are short and overhead it low—that means you get your parts quickly and the prices are right.

Yogi's Parts List:

PN MAG10701	Exhaust; Hot Rod Kit; 2.25-inch
PN MAG14215	Muffler; Oval Center/Center; 2.25-inch
PN Wl200	Power Window Lift Kit, Two-Door
PN HCC2	Hideaway Cup Caddy
PN NE5100FP	Windshield Wiper, 1951 Ford Passenger
PN 4050BS	Headlamp System; '40s and '50s; 7-inch Frenched
PN SHAVED	Shaved Door Handles-Existing Motors
PN SS1550	Door Poppers; 30 pound; Satin Aluminum
PN SW-D04	Trunk Lid Latch; 2-1/2x3-5/16 inches
PN IJ-DB	Inside Job Door Release, Billet
PN IJ-TB	Inside Job Trunk Release, Billet
PN SRS430	Trunk Latch and Striker Kit Bottom Mt
PN LEC71000	Steering Wheel Mark 10, Painted
PN LEC3722	Horn Button; Billet Groovy, Small
PN BLT55220	License Frame; With Light, Polished
PN BLT31120	Hub Adapter; 67-94 GM, Polished
PN BLK75125	Radiator Cap; 16 pound; Aluminum, Notch Grip; Black Anodized
PN BLK77109	Overflow Tank; 8.75-inch, Smooth Black
PN JU30102	Horn; Chrome/Black
PN ICANKIT	iPod Kit; For Use With Sass; Will Charge iPod Also
PN 7-0504	Line Clamp; 1/2-inch Single; Pol SS
PN NE-45	Fuel Hose; 12-inch Formed; 2-inch ID, 45-degree
PN Wl200	Power Window Lift Kit, Two-Door
PN EPWS-GM	Power Window Switch GM Spline
PN MAG10701	Exhaust; Hot Rod Kit; 2.25 inch
PN MAG14215	Muffler; Oval Center/Center; 2.25 inch
PN XSP-S975	Battery; XS Power 1600 Max Amp 500 Cold Cranking Amps
PN AAW500723	Battery Cable Kit; Trunk Mount, Top Post
PN FN-6y	Jumper Cable Connection; Remote, Black
PN FP-5y	Jumper Cable Connection; Remote, Red
PN 0 HRI5000	Bracket; Remote Battery Jumper Post Frame
PN SPC7365	Transmission Cooler; Dual Pass 12 inch, Aluminum
PN DEC250AK	Electric Exhaust Cut-Out Kit; 2.5 inch; With Hook Up Kit
PN 600-6624-00	Brake Line Kit - SS w/Thru Frame Ft
PN RL100	Latch; Rotary Type, Remote Release
PN DR-2	Door Release Actuator With Hardware
PN FWC-BA	Flex Conduits With Aluminum Ends

VINTAGE AIR
Air Conditioning Options

When it comes to equipping a street rod with air conditioning, thanks to Vintage Air there are lots of options.

GEN IV MAGNUM™
Universal Fit Systems

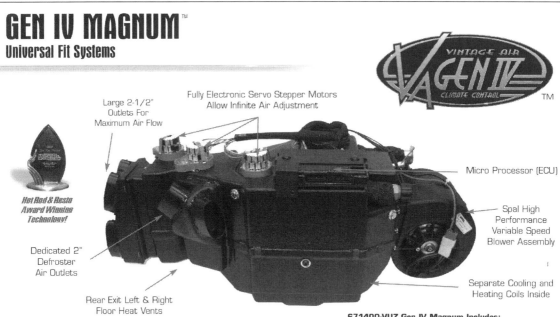

Large 2-1/2" Outlets For Maximum Air Flow

Fully Electronic Servo Stepper Motors Allow Infinite Air Adjustment

Hot Rod & Resto Award Winning Technology!

Dedicated 2" Defroster Air Outlets

Rear Exit Left & Right Floor Heat Vents

Micro Processor (ECU)

Spal High Performance Variable Speed Blower Assembly

Separate Cooling and Heating Coils Inside

671400-VUZ Gen IV Magnum Includes:
Evaporator unit, Mounting brackets, Wiring harness, Electric servo heater control valve, Duct hoses. Drain kit.

671400-VUZ - Gen IV Magnum - Heat, Cool & Defrost Model.

GEN-IV TECHNOLOGY DELIVERS OEM QUALITY CLIMATE CONTROL!
Enjoy true OEM style bi-level, infinitely adjustable, comfort in your classic car. This Gen IV Magnum system can handle even the largest sedan or wagon.

Controls are ordered separately - see next page.

Under hood components such as Compressor, Brackets, Condenser, Hose kit, Drier, and Optional upgrades are ordered separately from other sections in this catalog - see index on page 3.

Gen IV Magnum Features:

- Fully electronic operation - no cables or vacuum controls
- Micro-processor controlled coil temperature monitor - no capillary tube to install!
- Separate high capacity heat and cool coils
- Aluminum plate/fin A/C coil - most efficient evaporator design available
- Copper/brass CuproBraze™ parallel flow heater coil
- In full A/C mode air bypasses heater core resulting in less restriction and increased airflow.
- Servo blend air door for instant temperature adjustment
- Infinite dash/floor air blend
- Infinite defrost/floor air blend with dedicated defrost
- Variable speed blower motor
- Positive shut off solenoid-operated heater control valve in max A/C mode
- Multiple control panel options

Notice the unique shape of the Gen IV Magnum allows fitments in vehicles with higher transmission tunnels and stepped firewalls such as cars of the '50s and later.

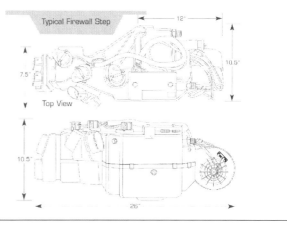

Typical Firewall Step

Top View

❯ *Vintage Air supplies measurements for all their units to make selecting one for the space available easy. Another option is the use of mock-up cases Vintage Air has available.*

GEN IV CONTROLS
Universal Fit Systems

Upgrade 3 Lever Gen IV ProLine™ Rectangular Panel

NEW!

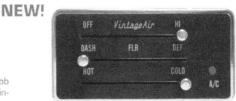

491230
Polished bezel and knobs (shown)

491231
All black anodized face and knobs

Includes label plates for horizontal or vertical mounting!

Machined aluminum slide control panel features a polished bezel and knobs with a matte finish mylar face. Also available in black anodized satin finish panels include mylar face for horizontal and vertical configurations and includes our exclusive soft white LED illumination. Panel measures 4.30" x 2.17".

Gen IV 3 Knob Base Under Dash Control
492050 - Super compact, easy to mount 3-knob control panel delivers valuable control at your fingertips. Individual switches can be removed from pod and mounted directly into your dash for increased design options and flexibility.
Pod measures 5.25" x 1.25"

(Individual rotary switches can be removed from the pod and mounted directly into your dash. Custom knob options are shown on page 54)

Upgrade 3 Knob Gen IV ProLine™ Oval Panels

Machined aluminum rotary control panel features a polished face and knobs with engraved icons. Also available in black anodized satin finish. Panels include our exclusive soft-white LED lighting in each knob. Panels measure 4.125" x 1.25".

Aluminum Knobs Are Back- Lit! Looks Cool!

491210-RUA - Horizontal
Polished Face and Knobs

491223-RUA - Horizontal
Anodized Face and Knobs

491214-RVA - Vertical
Polished Face and Knobs

491226-RVA - Vertical
Anodized Face and Knobs

❱ Vintage Air offers control panels for virtually any interior design.

UNDER DASH SYSTEMS
Universal Systems

13.5" Approx. With Motor

5.75"

15.5"

All Steel Case!
Original Mark IV Tooling!

THE REAL STEEL MARK IV IS BACK!

Vintage Air has created an exact reproduction of the most popular under dash air conditioner ever made. The Mark IV features an all steel case built from the original tooling. The timeless look of chrome and real steel combined with Vintage Air's proven performance makes the new Mark IV a great choice for your period perfect ride. Includes mounting brackets and drain line.

672001-VHY Mark IV - Under Dash Cool Only System.

SLIM LINE SYSTEMS - These value priced systems have been engineered to provide excellent cooling capacity and air delivery in a compact under dash package. They feature built-in controls and louvers.

11301-VUY-A Cool only (passenger side fittings)
11301-VUX-A Heat & Cool (passenger side fittings)
11300-VUZ-A Heat, Cool, Defrost

11401-VUY-A Cool only-black louvers (passenger side side fittings)
11401-VUX-A Heat & Cool-black louvers (passenger side fittings)
11400-VUZ-A Heat, Cool, Defrost-black louvers

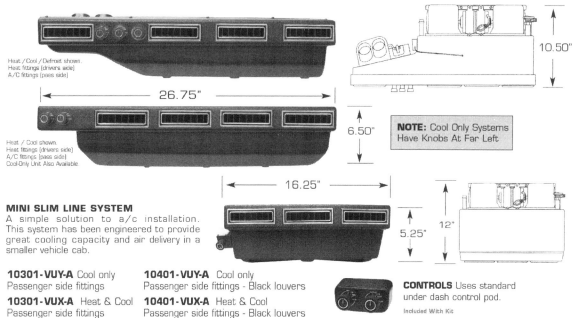

Heat / Cool / Defrost shown.
Heat fittings (drivers side)
A/C fittings (pass side)

10.50"

26.75"

Heat / Cool shown.
Heat fittings (drivers side)
A/C fittings (pass side)
Cool-Only Unit Also Available.

6.50"

NOTE: Cool Only Systems Have Knobs At Far Left

16.25"

MINI SLIM LINE SYSTEM

A simple solution to a/c installation. This system has been engineered to provide great cooling capacity and air delivery in a smaller vehicle cab.

5.25"

12"

10301-VUY-A Cool only
Passenger side fittings

10301-VUX-A Heat & Cool
Passenger side fittings

10401-VUY-A Cool only
Passenger side fittings - Black louvers

10401-VUX-A Heat & Cool
Passenger side fittings - Black louvers

CONTROLS Uses standard under dash control pod.
Included With Kit

❱ The new retro Mark IV underdash A/C unit is perfect for '50s and '60s cars. Other underdash units have A/C and heat.

LOUVERS
Under Dash Louvers & Controls

Universal Under Dash Louver Panels

2 piece louver set works well with any flat under dash installation. Includes ball louvers.

492000-VUA

3.625" Deep

3.375"   5.25" Deep

These Pods Include Louvers

4.75"

32"

3.25"

49050-VUL Under dash louver
For 2.5" hose.
49350-VUL All black for 2.5" hose.
49250-VUL Under dash louver
For 3" hose.

49059-VUL Under dash louver
For 2.5" hose.
49359-VUL All black louver
For 2.5" hose.

63016-VUL Double louver assembly 11.375" x 2.5". For 2.5" hose.
63316-VUL (All black)
63017-VUL Double louver assembly 11.375" x 2.5". For 2" hose.
63317-VUL (All black)

49051-VUL Left kick panel louver for 2.5" hose.
49361-VUL All black for 2.5" hose.
49251-VUL Left kick panel louver for 3" hose.

49151-VUL Right kick panel louver for 2.5" hose.
49351-VUL All black for 2.5" hose.
49252-VUL Right kick panel louver for 3" hose.

Under Dash Control & Louver Panels

492008 Clean and easy panel system for '32 Ford style dash applications. contour molded control panel mounts center louver and 4-knob Gen II rotary controls into a single neat package. Rotary switches and louver included. Standard textured finish.

Under Dash Center Louver Panels

Application-specific under dash center louver and housing panels for use with in-dash controls. Louver included.

49132-VFL 1928-32 Ford
49332-VFL (All black)

49137-VFL 1937 Ford and 1930-35 Chevy
49337-VFL (All black)

49134-VFL 1933-34 Ford
49334-VFL (All black)

49135-VFL 1935-36 Ford
49335-VFL (All black)

49100-VFL Flat Universal
49300-VFL (All black)

Universal Under Dash Louver Panels

472213 Control panel and 2.875" ball louver under dash pod. Uses 3 or 4 knob controls (not included) 12" x 3" Standard textured finish

47210-SHA Gen II Under dash pod w/louver for 4 Lever Gen II system controls using our servo heater control valve. Standard textured finish

472030-PFE '32 Ford Gen II under dash bare pod. Stamped for 49063-VUQ louver and 491200-RUA controls (not included). Standard textured finish

47211-SHA Gen II under dash pod for 4 Lever panel (For Gen II systems with servo heater valve). Standard textured finish

❯ Dash outlets are available in a wide array of styles and sizes.

LOUVERS
Standard Series - ProLine Series

NOTE: All louvers are sold individually.

49052-VUL 5.25" x 2.5"
For 2.5" hose.
49352-VUL (All black)

49327-VUL 3.875" x 2"
For 2.5" hose. (All black)

49057-VUL 4.75" x 1.562"
for 2.5" hose.
49325-VUL (All black)

49056-VUL 3.875" x 1.562" for 2.5" hose.
49356-VUL (All black)
49156-VUL 3.875" x 1.562" for 2" hose.
49326-VUL (All black)

49066-VUL 90° Angle flow louvers.
3.88" x 1.57"w/chrome trim.
49366-VUL 90° Angle w/black trim.

49067-VUL 90° Angle flow louvers.
4.75" x 1.57" w/chrome trim
49367-VUL 90° Angle w/black trim.

490535 Double vane
louver chrome. For 2.5" hose.

499195 SlimLine Adjustable
Double Vane Louver.
Thru-dash mount. 3" diameter
(requires 2 5/8" Hole size)
Note: Louver Open, Close & Rotate 360°

49054-VUL
Underdash For 2.5" hose.
49354-VUL
Underdash (All black)
49154-VUL
Underdash (All chrome)
49154-VUL
Underdash (All chrome)
49051-VUI
Underdash louver pod only
(Fits all 2.875" Louvers)

— 6 7/8" —
4"
— 3" —

490500 Through Kick
Panel Louver Pod.
Louver mounts through
the backside of kick panel.
Includes 49053-VUL Louver
and installation template.
(Sold individually)

49053-VUL Thru-dash mount.
2.875" Dia. For 2.5" hose.
49353-VUL Thru-dash mount (All black)
49153-VUL Thru-dash mount (All chrome)
49049-VUL Thru-dash mount. For 3" hose.

499194 Adjustable Double Vane Louver.
Chrome bezel thru-dash mount.
2.706" diameter.
499193 Adjustable Double Vane Louver.
Black bezel thru-dash mount.
2.706" diameter.
Note: Louver Open, Close & Rotate 360°

Professional Quality Roto Broach Hole Saw
421002 The right way to cut louver mounting holes in metals, plastics, or wood trim. Includes pilot and arbor. 2.625 Diameter - 3/8" Drill shank size.

Vintage Air ProLine™ Series
Upgrade Louvers

49058-VUQ
Rectangle louver
with billet trim.
4.25" x 2" Face size

49062-VUQ Streamline louver. Polished
aluminum trim. 4" x 1.75" Face size
490621 Black anodized trim with
black vanes (shown)

49203-VUQ Brushed aluminum rectangle
louver. 4"x 1.25" Face size (Above)
49202-VUQ Brushed aluminum rectangle
louver. 6"x 1.25" Face size (Left)

49063-VUQ Streamline louver.
Polished aluminum trim. (shown)
4.875" x 1.75" Face size
490622 Black anodized trim
with black vanes

❯ Dash outlets are available in a wide array of styles and sizes.

NEW DESIGNS!

Vintage Air
ProLine™ Series
Upgrade Louvers

LOUVERS
ProLine Series Upgrade Louvers

ProLine Penta Louvers
499120 Clear Anodized Louver
499121 Black Anodized Louver
2.625" Diameter

ProLine LoPro Penta Louvers
499160 Clear Anodized Louver
499161 Black Anodized Louver
2.625" Diameter

ProLine Rotary Vane Louvers
499119 Clear Anodized Louver
499112 Black Anodized Louver
2.625" Diameter

ProLine Tridant Louvers
499124 Clear Anodized Louver
499125 Black Anodized Louver
2.625" Diameter

ProLine Saturn Tridant Louvers
499162 Clear Anodized Louver
499163 Black Anodized Louver
2.875" Diameter

ProLine Spyder Louvers
499122 Clear Anodized Louver
499123 Black Anodized Louver
2.625" Diameter

ProLine Planar Louvers
499210 Clear Anodized Louver
499211 Black Anodized Louver
2.625" Diameter

ProLine Saturn Planar Louvers
499164 Clear Anodized Louver
499165 Black Anodized Louver
499159 Black Anodized Ball With Polished Bezel
2.875" Diameter

Slyder Series Louvers
49215-VUQ Clear
Anodized Machined
All Aluminum
2.750" Diameter

ProLine Venturi Louvers
49212-VUQ All Aluminum
Machined Bezel And Ball
2.875" Diameter

ProLine StreamLine Round Louvers
Injection Molded Inner Ball
49054-VUQ Polished Aluminum Bezel
490541 Black Anodized Aluminum Bezel
2.875" Diameter

ProLine Round Louvers
49053-VUQ Black
Injection Molded Ball
With Machined
Aluminum Bezel
2.901" Diameter

ProLine Oval Louvers
491902 Chrome Plated
Die Cast Housing With
Injection Molded
Directional Vanes
4.00" x 1.60"

❱ *Dash outlets are available in a wide array of styles and sizes.*

❯ A California Car Cover was used to protect the AMSOIL/STREET RODDER Road Tour '51 from the elements after a long day on the road.

❯ California Car Covers are available in custom fit and universal designs in materials suitable for indoor, outdoor, or a combination of environments.

GOLDEN SHINE

The maintenance of any street rod is an ongoing process and the "care and feeding" of the paint, wheels, tires, and glass is never ending—especially if you enjoy the drive. We have included a number of California Shine products, introduced by California Car Cover, which will take care of every facet of your street rod to make sure it looks (and shines) its best.

Cream Wax

Golden Shine Cream Wax is gentle and unbelievably simple to use, without sacrificing optimal results. The unique formula offers unparalleled protection and a deep, glossy shine, thanks to a special blend of resins, polymers, and 100 percent pure Brazilian carnauba wax. Safe for all finishes, it never stains trim or leaves a white residue. Apply this wax anywhere; it's safe to use in the sun and the shade.

Paint Polish

Ultimate Paint Polish was designed as a fine machine polish and gloss enhancer. Golden Shine's Ultimate Paint Polish will gently, and safely, eliminate light paint imperfections for a deep, glossy finish. Safe for all use on all finishes and designed for use by the casual and experienced detailer, Ultimate Paint Polish is the premiere choice for a finishing polish in order to obtain

the brightest possible shine. Use Golden Shine's color-coded "green" polishing pad with an orbital polisher, such as the Porter Cable 7424xp, for the best solution in paint finishing. It's designed as a fine polishing pad to deftly remove light paint imperfections to provide a deep glossy finish. Measuring 7-1/2 inches and designed with a special hex patter, this pad provides superior correction and longevity.

Swirl Remover Machine Polish

The Golden Shine Swirl Remover Machine Polish is the perfect way to remove stubborn paint scratches and swirl marks without risking damage to the vehicle's paint. Designed for use by both the casual and seasoned detailer, Swirl Remover is specially formulated to provide the best and safest paint correction possible. Using only the finest alumina abrasives that work longer and provide superior lubrication in order to safely remove swirl marks, water spotting, light scratches, and oxidation.

Use Golden Shine's color-coded "orange" polishing pad with an orbital polisher, such as the Porter Cable 7424xp, for safe and superior paint correction. This pad is designed as a medium cutting pad and eliminates tough swirl makes, water spots, oxidation, and paint imperfections. Measuring 7-1/2 inches and designed with a special hex pattern, this pad provides superior correction and longevity.

Golden Shine Sparkling Glaze Hand Polish

The Sparkling Glaze Hand Polish by Golden Shine is a fine polish that will reduce spider-like scratches and blemishes from your paint and achieve a smooth, supremely glassy finish. A unique blend of lubricants, essential oils, and mild diminishing abrasives qualifies Sparkling Glaze Hand Polish as the perfect way to remove light swirl marks and oxidation. Formulated to be extremely easy to use and remove; simply apply with Golden Shine's color-matched microfiber applicator and wipe off with a microfiber towel. Safe for hand or machine application.

Quick Shine

Golden Shine Quick Shine instant detailer allows you to quickly and conveniently add depth and gloss to almost any surface while safely removing dust and dirt particles for that just-waxed look. Powered by gloss-enhancing polymers and lubricating oils to deliver a show-stopping shine between washes.

Metal Polish

Golden Shine Metal Polish will produce a stunning gloss that your street rod deserves. The proven formula clears away oxidation without scratching and restores a lustrous, gleaming finish to copper, brass, billet aluminum, stainless steel, nickel, chrome, and is also the perfect polish for your wheels. Restores brightness and provides long-lasting mirror-like protection.

Clean & Clear Glass Cleaner

Safe and ammonia-free, Golden Shine Clean & Clear contains no harsh chemicals and is 100 percent biodegradable and safe for the environment. An ultra-fine polishing agent is specially formulated to gently remove dirt and grime from glass or clear plastic, and leave windows streak- and smudge-free. Gentle enough for use on delicate window tint and navigation displays, but tough enough to clear grime and tough window buildup with ease.

Tire & Trim Dressing

Golden Shine Tire & Trim Dressing is the equivalent of 40-spf sunscreen, goes on easy and creates a beautiful, semi-gloss shine that lasts for

weeks. The water-based cream formula contains modern polymers that coat and bond to all vinyl and rubber for premium protection. It contains no alcohol or petroleum ingredients that can crack or dry your dash, tires, and other plastics. Specially designed to ensure an even application, the applicators are safe, gentle, easy to grip, and get right to the spot.

Brilliant Wheel Cleaner

Golden Shine Brilliant Wheel Cleaner will quickly and safely clean your street rod's wheels without any harsh chemicals. Safe for use on most wheel finishes, including clearcoated, painted, and anodized wheels. The formula contains no butyl or petroleum distillates, making it not only safe to use on your wheels, but also safe for the environment. To use, simply spray on and lightly agitate, and rinse away the built-up dirt and brake dust.

Wash & Wax

Golden Shine Wash & Wax is the best way to clean paint because it safely breaks up and encapsulates dirt within the lubricants to remove them without scratching. Some formulas aren't strong enough to break up dirt while others are too strong and strip wax right off. It breaks dust, dirt, and other contaminants loose and is safe for use on all surfaces. A unique blend of conditioners and synthetic gloss enhancers to rejuvenate your street rod's luster between waxing. The

pH neutral car wash is specially formulated to deliver the highest possible shine and minimize water spotting.

Go-To Cleaner & Degreaser

Golden Shine Go-To Cleaner & Degreaser contains wetting agents that produce a superior foaming action, strong enough to lift caked-on dirt and brake dust from wheels but safe enough to gently clean interior plastics, vinyl, and upholstery. The water-based formula is free from acids and cheap butyls found in most wheel cleaners that can cause wheel damage and pollute the environment.

Go-To Cleaner deep cleans tires, removing browning and old tire dressing, without leaching the tire's built-in wax protection. Used in full strength, it is great underhood to degrease your engine and effectively tackles the undercarriage, road tar, sap, bugs, and bird droppings. It's available in 16-ounce and 1-gallon sizes, making it convenient for a variety of projects.

Interior Cleaner

Golden Shine Interior Cleaner quickly and effectively tackles the toughest stains, and lifts dirt and oil from the interior of your vehicle. The spray cleaner is free from dyes and color-altering chemicals, so it's safe to use on upholstery, carpet, and headliners, as well as vinyl, plastic, and even leather—and virtually any surface in your street rod. Kind to the environment, the Interior Cleaner is a non-foaming, water-based spray on/wipe off formula that lifts grime and won't leave a stiff or sticky residue.

Maintainer Kit

This handy kit includes everything you need to keep that brilliant Golden Shine luster going between deep clean sessions, including a California Car Duster, a three pack of Quick Shine Premium Microfiber Towels and a two pack of Tire & Trim Applicators to use with the 16-ounce bottles (one each) of Quick Shine Instant Detailer for reviving that just-waxed look, Tire & Trim Dressing to restore vitality while protecting your dash and tires from cracking and drying, and Clean & Clear Glass to bring out the streak-free sparkle of windows and mirrors.

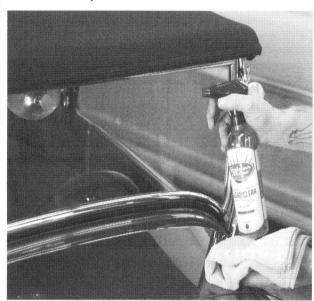

AUTOMOTIVE

DESCRIPTION

Dynaliner is an ultra-lightweight closed cell high-performance insulation. Dark gray in color, Dynaliner is available in 1/8", 1/4" and 1/2" thicknesses. Dynaliner is self-adhesive with a high-temperature acrylic adhesive. Dynaliner is optimized for temperatures from -30°F to 200°F (-34°C to 94°C) and meets both UL and FMVSS flame resistance.

ACOUSTIC AND THERMAL PROPERTIES

Dynaliner is the perfect ultra-lightweight insulator to use on top Dynamat. This durable, crush and tear resistant material has the highest heat blocking properties available in a single layer synthetic foam-type material. Dynaliner is not affected by oil and does not absorb water.

APPLICATION

Easy to install, Dynaliner provides acoustic isolation and excellent thermal insulation for roof, interior firewall, floor, quarter panels, doors and even under hood. Dynaliner can be used in place of carpet pad.

INSTALLATION

Cutting: Dynaliner can be cut to a desired size and shape with a pair of scissors or razor knife. Dynaliner is self-adhesive. Make sure area is free from dirt oil and debris. For best results, work evenly from one side to the other applying even pressure.

AVAILABLE SIZES

Dimensions: 32" x 54" (81cm x 137cm)
Coverage: 12.0 ft² (1.1m²)
Available 1/8", 1/4" and 1/2" (3mm, 6mm and 6mm) thickness

TYPICAL MATERIAL PROPERTIES*

Part#	11101	11102	11103
Material Thickness:	0.125 in.(3.18mm)	0.250 in.(6.35mm)	0.500 in.(12.70mm)
Weight:	0.042lb./ft² (0.21kg/m²)	0.084lb./ft² (0.41kg/m²)	0.168lb./ft² (0.82kg/m²)
Density:	4.0lb./ft³ (64.6kg/m³)	4.0lb./ft³ (64.6kg/m³)	4.0lb./ft³ (64.6kg/m³)
Adhesive Strength:	tba	tba	tba
Tensile Strength:	tba	tba	tba
Tear Strength:	tba	tba	tba
Temperature Range: (Maximum)	-30°F to 200°F (-34°C to 93°C)	-30°F to 200°F (-34°C to 93°C)	-30°F to 200°F (-34°C to 93°C)
Temperature Range: (Optimal)	-30°F to 200°F (-34°C to 93°C)	-30°F to 200°F (-34°C to 93°C)	-30°F to 200°F (-34°C to 93°C)
STC:	N/A	N/A	N/A
FMVSS302:	Meets	Meets	Meets
UL Rating:	UL 94 HF-1	UL 94 HF-1	UL 94 HBF
R Value:	0.42°Fft²hr/Btu (0.07Km²hr/W)	0.83°Fft²hr/Btu (0.15Km²hr/W)	1.7°Fft²hr/Btu (0.3Km²hr/W)

* Material properties have tolerances of ±10% unless otherwise noted
  Parentheses denote metric measurements.

The data provided in the material summary are typical of average values based on testing conducted by Dynamic Control or independent laboratories. They are indicative only of the results obtained in such tests and should be used for reference only. Materials used in situations not recommended must be tested under actual service to determine their suitability for that purpose.

DYNAMIC CONTROL
3042 Symmes Road • Hamilton, Ohio 45015
phone: 1-800-225-8133 • fax: 1-800-873-2423 • www.dynamat.com

DESCRIPTION

Dynamat Xtreme is a patented, light-weight, elastomeric, butyl and aluminum constrained-layer vibrational damper. Dynamat Xtreme conforms and fuses easily to sheet metal and other hard substrates. Material performance is optimized for temperature ranges between -10°C to +60°C (14°F to +140°F). Material can withstand temperature extremes between -54°C to +149°C (-65°F to +300°F) and is highly resistant to aging.

ACOUSTIC PROPERTIES

The acoustic loss factor "n" is used as a measure of ability to damp structure-borne sound. It states how much vibrational energy (in steel sheets for instance) is converted to heat rather than sound. For constructions containing several layers of damping material, the combined loss factor "n comb" is used. The theoretical maximum loss factor is 1 (no vibration). An undamped 1mm thick steel panel has a loss factor of roughly 0.001 at 200 Hz. Dynamat Xtreme applied to that panel would increase the loss factor to 0.417 @ +20°C (+68°F). Multiple layers of Dynamat Xtreme can be used to improve sound damping further.

APPLICATIONS

Dynamat Xtreme can be die cut to shape and placed onto the body surface after sheet metal cleaning operation and prior to paint system (typically at the sealer application operation) or on painted panels. Dynamat Xtreme is used as treatment for metal panels, partitions, ducts, doors, bins, panels etc. in railroad cars, buses, automobiles and ships. It is also used for ventilation ducts, relay cabinets, steel furniture, home appliances, sink units, computer equipment, machine tools and for many other purposes.

INSTALLATION

Dynamat Xtreme should be cut to the desired size before the release liner is removed. It may be cut with scissors, knife or die. Remove dust, grease, moisture, and other foreign matter from the application surface. Peel off the release liner. The simplest application technique is to bend the mat slightly and attach it along its shortest edge. The mat is then pressed firmly into place, preferably with a roller for larger pieces. This reduces the risk of leaving air pockets, which reduce the sound damping capacity. The temperature of the mat and application surface should not be below room temperature during fitting. Heating the material is not necessary.

SPECIFICATIONS

Appearance:
Black butyl based core with 4 mil aluminum constraining layer, craft paper release liner

Thickness:
0.067" (1.7mm)

Mass:
0.45lbs./ft.^{2} (2.20kg/m^2)

Acoustic Loss Factor @ Temperature (Using ASTM method E756 @ 200 Hz):

0.081 @ +14°F (-10°C)
0.240 @ +32°F (+0°C)
0.257 @ +50°F (+10°C)
0.417 @ +68°F (+20°C)
0.259 @ +86°F (+30°C)
0.194 @ +104°F (+40°C)
0.140 @ +122°F (+50°C)
0.094 @ +140°F (+60°C)

Temperature Range (Optimal Performance):
14°F to +140°F (-10°C to +60°C)

Temperature Range (Resistance):
-65°F to +300°F (-54°C to +149°C)

Adhesive Peel Strength:
42.6 lb./in. (74.8 N/cm) on cold steel

Chemical Resistance:
Resistant to water and mineral oils

Federal Standards Tests:
FMVSS 302: *Meets*

Handling And Application:
Material must be stored at room temperature for best application

Storage Information:
Number Of Sheets In Stack: 50 max
Material must be stored horizontally in its wrapping

DYNAMIC CONTROL
3042 Symmes Road • Hamilton, Ohio 45015
phone: **1-800-225-8133** • *fax:* **1-800-873-2423** • **www.dynamat.com**

© 2001 Dynamic Control of North America, Inc.
Part No. 2204

REFERENCE CHART

4" x 10" XTREME DYNAMAT

Coverage: 0.28 ft.^{2} (0.03m^2)
Weight: 0.12 lbs. (0.05 kg)
Dimensions: 4"x10"
(100mm x 254mm)

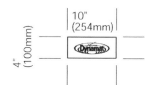

10" x 10" XTREME DYNAMAT

Coverage: 0.69 ft.^{2} (0.06m^2)
Weight: 0.31 lbs. (0.14 kg)
Dimensions: 10"x10"
(254mm x 254mm)

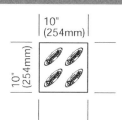

18" x 32" XTREME DYNAMAT

Coverage: 4.0 ft.^{2} (0.37m^2)
Weight: 1.80 lbs. (0.82 kg)
Dimensions: 18"x32"
(457mm x 812mm)

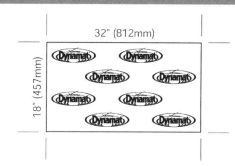

12" x 36" XTREME DYNAMAT

Coverage: 3.00 ft.^{2} (0.28m^2)
Weight: 1.35 lbs. (0.61 kg)
Dimensions: 12"x36"
(305mm x 914mm)

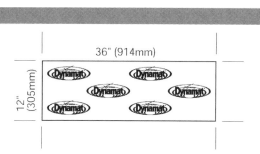

LUBRICATION FOR THE LONG HAUL

AMSOIL INC. Synthetics

Every year our Road Tour cars put on lots of miles in a very short period of time—rolling the odometer up to numbers between 20,000-25,000 miles in a summer is typical. There isn't much time for maintenance and absolutely none for breakdowns. In addition, these cars are always equipped with high-performance engines, driveline, and chassis components that require the best in lubricants, which is why we continue to use AMSOIL INC. synthetic products exclusively.

Synthetic oil has actually been around for quite some time, with the earliest attempts at production being made prior to 1900. The next big push in research was a result of Germany's oil shortage during World War II. It prompted intense investigation into the possibilities of creating synthetic lubricants. In fact, from 1944 on, 10 percent of the oil produced in that country was synthetic. However, it was the needs of jet engines that ushered in the new era of synthetics; long duration, high-speed operation, as well as huge variations in operating temperatures demanded performance beyond the scope of conventional oils. Synthetic oil was the answer to that need.

Part Numbers of AMSOIL INC. Products Used:

AMOQT	10W-40 high zinc synthetic oil
EAO24	oil filter
ATFQT	Synthetic ATF
GLCSC	Synthetic multi-purpose spray grease
GWRCR	Synthetic water resistant grease
AMHSC	Heavy-duty metal protector
APICN	Performance Improver (P.I.)
AMPSC	Metal protector spray

One of the big concerns in performance automotive circles is the reformulation of engine oil, specifically the reduction in zinc levels. To get answers to some of the most commonly asked questions we went to the experts at AMSOIL INC.

Q: What is the purpose of zinc additives?
A: Zinc-based additives are used primarily as anti-wear agents to prevent premature wear of engine components. Zinc dialkyldithiophosphate (ZDDP) is the most commonly utilized form, which also provides corrosion and oxidation protection.

Q: Why were zinc levels lowered?
A: Zinc levels were lowered in response the American Petroleum Institute (API) SM and International Lubricants Standardization and Approval Committee (ILSAC) GF-4 oil specifications. The action was driven by original equipment manufacturers (OEM) based on

the Environmental Protection Agency (EPA) mandate that emission reduction systems needed to function for a specific period of time without failing. OEM pushed to remove anything that was in motor oils that could potentially harm emissions reduction systems.

Q: What API designations have reduced zinc?
A: There has been a stepwise reduction in sulfur and phosphorus in API oil specification designations, which drove the reduction in ZDDP content. The current API SM gasoline motor oil specification limits phosphorus to a maximum of 0.085 percent. Sulfur is limited to a maximum of 0.50 percent for 0W-20, 0W-30, 5W-20, 5W-30, and 0.70 percent for 10W-30 viscosity categories.

Q: What problems does reduced zinc create?
A: Reduced zinc or ZDDP content has been linked to issues with premature wear in flat-tappet camshaft engines and, in particular, with engines that include high-tension valvesprings or other modifications, which create high contact pressures.

❯ AMSOIL INC. Z-Rod Synthetic Motor Oil meets API-SL and earlier specifications, allowing for the increased levels of anti-wear additives. It's recommended for a maximum drain interval of 5,000 miles/one year, or 3,000 miles/one year on heavily modified vehicles.

Q: *Are there other additives in your oil that provide the same protection as zinc?*
A: AMSOIL INC. markets and sells some motor oils that contain additive packages that replace a portion of the ZDDP component. These motor oils provide great anti-wear protection to the targeted applications. Street rodders and classic car enthusiasts many times need or prefer the extra anti-wear protection provided by motor oils containing high levels of ZDDP. For this reason, AMSOIL INC. continues to provide the Premium Protection line of motor oils, which have higher levels of ZDDP for these specific applications.

Q: *For new engines do you recommend specific break-in additives?*
A: AMSOIL INC. does not currently provide any break-in additives. The use of a break-in additive during the break-in period only (as opposed to an ongoing treatment) is advisable in conjunction with a high-quality lubricant for flat-tappet cams. The break-in period is when flat-tappet cams are most vulnerable to failure. We also recommend that street rodders use a high-quality assembly lubricant. (Talk to the manufacturer of your camshaft engine.)

Q: *Do you recommend any oil additives for normal operation?*
A: AMSOIL INC. does not recommend using any oil additives. If the motor oil is formulated correctly for the application, there is no need to consider use of any oil additives. Formulation of motor oils is a difficult balancing act. Oil additives focused on extreme pressure or anti-wear

❯ *AMSOIL INC. Synthetic 10W-40 motor oil provides the extra anti-wear protection required by engines with flat-tappet cams and high-tension valvesprings.*

resistance may appear to initially help with these particular properties but upset the balance in other areas and can promote acidic corrosion, excessive oxidation, and foam, for example.

Q: *Many engine builders recommend the use of diesel oil in vintage/flat-tappet engines. Is that a viable option?*
A: The assumption is that diesel oils contain high levels of ZDDP, which cannot be found in other motor oils. This recommendation is partially correct. First, make sure that the diesel oil carries gasoline credentials; some do not. If the diesel oil is recommended for gasoline use and it contains a healthy dose of ZDDP, it may be a viable option. Be very careful not to generalize that all diesel oils contain high levels of ZDDP; this is not the case! Modern API CJ-4 type oils have lower levels of ZDDP than their predecessors. If an oil is in question, send a sample to a reputable oil analysis testing service for a metals analysis. Oils containing over 1,100 ppm of phosphorus indicate sufficient levels of anti-wear protection. AMSOIL INC. recommends oil analyzers, which can be accessed at oaitesting.com.

Q: *Are racing oils subject to lowered zinc levels?*
A: The low phosphorus levels as required by API SM apply only to 0W-20 through 10W-30 viscosity ranges. Racing oils are typically higher viscosity and anything above a 30 weight is not required to have low levels of phosphorus, even if it is API SM. Most racing oils are expected to contain

❯ *AMSOIL INC. Synthetic Multi-Vehicle Automatic Transmission Fluid is engineered to outperform conventional automatic transmission fluids. It's recommended for transmissions, hydraulics, power steering, and other applications.*

high levels of anti-wear protection since durability is their main purpose. AMSOIL INC. racing oils contain high levels of ZDDP.

Q: *Are racing oils a good option for street-driven performance engines? Why or why not?*
A: That is dependent on the brand and formulation. Racing oils designed exclusively for the track many times do not contain appropriate levels of detergents and dispersants required for longer-term street use. These formulations would not provide adequate protection against engine sludge, rust, oxidation, and attack from acids and other combustion by-products. The best advice is to talk with a reputable manufacturer, ask informed questions, and make decisions based on the actual specifications.

Q: *In oils with lowered zinc levels, do higher viscosities provide any better protection?*
A: Higher viscosity oils may help somewhat with extra protection, but with flat-tappet camshaft engine applications, especially with modifications, including high-tension valvesprings, a strong antiwear package is required to protect your investment.

Q: *What do you recommend for oil change intervals?*
A: Oil change intervals are dependent on the engine modifications and fuel used.

❱ ▧ AMSOIL INC. Metal Protector (MP) and AMSOIL INC. Heavy Duty Metal Protector (MPHD) are spray-on products that protect metal surfaces, displace water, and silence squeaks. MP cuts through rust and corrosion to restore free movement of "frozen" hardware parts. MPHD lubricates metal surfaces, leaving a dry wax-like film.

If an engine is heavily modified, it will operate hotter than normal and require more frequent change intervals. Non-pump gas can also promote faster oil degradation. Generally speaking, if using high-quality synthetic motor oil, such as AMSOIL INC., and using standard pump gas, changing the oil within 3,000- to 5,000-mile intervals is safe.

Q: *Many street rods are parked for extended lengths during the winter, what are your suggestions to protect their engines?*
A: Change your oil before you park your baby for the winter and make sure to use a well-balanced oil that you can count on to protect your investment from corrosion while it hibernates. Spraying fogging oil down the intake system is also a good idea. Damage from rust and corrosion due to long periods in storage is an issue common to classic and vintage cars, which spend much of their existence in storage. AMSOIL INC. Z-Rod Synthetic Motor Oil is formulated with a unique blend of rust and corrosion inhibitors to ensure maximum protection during hibernation.

Q: *For flat-tappet engines, particularly older high-performance engines with higher than stock valvespring pressures, which of your oils would you recommend?*
A: AMSOIL INC. Premium Protection 10W-40 (AMO) and 20W-50 (ARO) racing oil 20W-50 (TRO) are higher viscosity oils that contain high levels of phosphorus and zinc antiwear additives. AMSOIL INC. diesel oils, 5W-30 (HDD), and 10W-30 (ACD), are lower viscosity products qualified for gasoline engines that also contain high levels of ZDDP anti-wear additives. AMSOIL INC. Z-Rod is formulated with high levels of zinc dialkyldithiophosphate (ZDDP) that provides exceptional protection for flat-tappet cams, lifters, and rockers. ZDDP is a proven antiwear agent that is especially important in classic and performance vehicles with flat-tappet cams.

❱ AMSOIL INC. Synthetic Water Resistant Grease meets the highest performance standards set by the National Lubrication Grease Institute (NLGI), GC for wheel bearing applications and LB for chassis applications. It may be used in automotive wheel bearings, chassis or other applications for which an NLGI No. 2 GC or LB grease is recommended.

GOING FROM POINT A TO B WITH INTERCITY LINES

Thanks in part to the Internet, it's not unusual to buy or sell a car from one side of the country and ship it to the other. Then there are those rodders who send their cars to a distant shop for custom work, or vacationers who drive one way to an event and have the car transported the other. At one time moving a valuable car for any reason was a risky proposition, but today, it's practical, safe, and economical, thanks to Intercity Lines.

Intercity Lines started as a small, family owned business and has evolved into the nation's premier enclosed automotive transporter, thanks to the special care they give their customers' vehicles. They tell us the key to safe and secure transport of a car is proper equipment, preparation, and attention to detail.

To ensure a vehicle receives the best care possible during shipping, the pros at Intercity Lines suggest you think about the following when considering a transport company:

Reputation: It's always best to work with a known company, one with a proven track record and experience in moving special-interest vehicles. Visit websites. Get referrals. Check references. Do your homework.

Carrier versus Broker: Always work with a carrier direct. Avoid brokers. Make sure the carrier operates its own equipment—brokers don't.

Insurance: Make sure the carrier supplies a Certificate of Insurance, an agreement that states the insurance coverage as well as pick up and delivery times. Vehicles are typically insured for up to $1 million.

No Deposits: Never, never give a deposit. Legitimate carriers never ask for a deposit in advance; brokers typically do ask for a deposit. Another reason to avoid using a broker.

Tracking: Reputable companies know where their trucks—and your car—are at all times. All Intercity trucks are equipped with GPS tracking; a quick call to Intercity informs you of your vehicle's whereabouts.

Enclosed versus Open Trailer: Enclosed trailers provide maximum protection of a vehicle; it's why Intercity only uses enclosed trailers. Rain, sleet, snow, hail, sand, road debris can all damage vehicles left exposed to the elements. Moreover, cars hauled in enclosed trailers are secure against vandalism.

Lift Gates versus Ramps: All Intercity trailers use hydraulic lift gates to load the vehicle into position. Vehicles with low ground clearance—exotic sports cars, lowered street rods, vintage race cars—can be damaged driving up a ramp. In addition, if a vehicle is transported often, moving up and down a ramp can strain the vehicle's driveline. Yes, clutches have been smoked on the short trip up a loading ramp.

❱ *Intercity transporters are fully enclosed and fitted with hydraulic lift gates to ensure maximum safety in loading. This keeps the car level at all times, eliminating any driveline strain or undercarriage damage.*

Inoperable Vehicles: Often, cars in various stages of restoration or construction need to be shipped. No problem. Wrap spare or loose parts carefully and put them inside the car or the trunk if they will fit securely and not hamper the view from inside or risk damaging the vehicle. Extra wheels and tires can also be shipped with the car for a modest extra charge.

Winch Availability: If a vehicle is not driveable, or if its brakes are inoperable, the transporter should use a winch to move the car on and off the truck in the safest possible manner. However, if the trailer is equipped with lift gates—as are all of Intercity's—the vehicle can be pushed onto the gate, then into the trailer.

When preparing a car to be transported the following steps should be taken:

Gas Tank: Vehicles should be transported with a quarter tank or less of gasoline in the tank. This is not only safer, it makes for a lighter vehicle. A gallon of gas weighs just under 7 pounds, so a full tank can significantly increase the overall transport weight.

Check the Antifreeze: Many vehicles based in Florida, Arizona, or Texas may be running straight water in their cooling systems. Of course, the temperature never drops below freezing in those states. However, if a car is being transported during winter to a cold-weather climate, that water could freeze in the engine block and/or radiator—with disastrous results. The solution is simple: Prior to shipment, flush the cooling system and fill it with the recommended blend of antifreeze and water.

Properly Secure or Remove Batteries: If not properly fastened, a battery can shift or dislodge during shipping, causing corrosive damage to wiring and sheetmetal. It could also be a fire hazard. It's also a good idea to disconnect the ground strap once the car is loaded into position.

Use the Cut-off Switch: If the car is equipped with a battery cut-off switch (many race cars have one), it should be placed to the "off" position to reduce electrical hazard. Naturally, remember to instruct the transport crew of the switch's location and operation.

Keep the Interior Free of Loose Items: The transport team needs a clear, unobstructed view from inside in order to move the vehicle safely. Exotic cars, for example, have a limited rearward view, so loading the car with personal items—that floor jack in the back seat—to save on outside shipping costs, decreases visibility even further. Moreover, such items are not covered by the transporting carrier's loss policy—only the consigned vehicle is insured against loss.

Check for Food or Perishables: Simply put, your car isn't a pantry or a fridge on wheels. Before shipping, be sure the car's interior is free of food. A Snickers can melt, a Coke can explode or puncture. Perishables can damage a vehicle.

❯ *Intercity was the first transport company in the United States to introduce and install the Qualcomm Satellite Tracking to indicate the exact location of their vehicles at all times and provides an extra measure of security.*

MILLER ELECTRIC MFG. CO.

Buying Your First Welder: A Practical, Informative Guide for Do-It-Yourselfers

You may be the creative type. Or, perhaps, you have the handy knack and are just looking to tinker around … building and fixing stuff. You might have your sights set on opening a small repair shop, a studio, or new gallery. You could be a farmer or rancher, classic car enthusiast, fabricator or woodworker … or you may just want to be able to repair or salvage something that is broken versus opting to toss it away.

Regardless of your interests, needs, or motivation, you're a do-it-yourselfer interested in buying your first welder.

Whether you already have previous welding experience, or, you're a welding novice, you are likely here because you need some help getting started. Miller Electric Mfg. Co. is dedicated to providing objective, informative, and practical information to assist you in making the appropriate choice.

Relax and read on. You've come to the right place!

Getting Started

Unfortunately, there is no single welding process suitable for all applications, so let's begin with an overview of the basic processes and highlight the capabilities and advantages of each. This will help us better match a process to your specific needs.

If you have previous welding experience, feel free to skip ahead. If you are somewhat of a novice, this section will provide you with a better understanding of the types of welders available, how each performs, and the degree of welding skill required to operate each. In addition, we'll offer examples of specific applications best suited to each process.

Matching your needs and welding skills with a specific process is critical before moving on to discuss specific welder model options.

Welding Processes

The most common welding processes include Stick, MIG/Flux-cored, and TIG. Each process has its own unique set of benefits and limitations, works well in some welding applications, and not well in others. There's no "one size fits all" — and as you will soon discover — for good reason.

Stick Welding: If you learned to weld years ago, you likely learned using an arc welder. Stick welding has, for many years, been the most popular method for most home-shop welding needs. Stick welding uses an electric current flowing from a gap between the metal and the welding stick, also known as an arc-welding electrode. Stick welding is an effective method for welding most alloys or joints and can be used both indoors and outdoors, or in drafty areas. It is also the most economical welding method and largely popular because of its ability to create an effective bond on rusty or dirty metals.

Arc welding is limited, however, to metals no thinner than 18-gauge and requires frequent rod changing, emits significant spatter, and welds must be cleaned upon completion. Stick welding is also more difficult to learn and use, particularly the ability to strike and maintain an arc. Arc welders are available in either AC or DC or AC/DC—with AC being the most economical. It is used for welding thicker metals of 1/16 inch or greater. They are a good choice for farmers, hobbyists, and home maintenance chores.

MIG Welding/Gas Metal Arc Welding (GMAW): MIG welders use a wire welding electrode on a spool that is fed automatically at a constant pre-selected speed. The arc, created by an electrical current between the base metal and the wire, melts the wire and joins it together with the base, producing a high-strength weld with great appearance and little need for cleaning. MIG welding is clean, easy, and can be used on either thin or thicker plate metals.

A slight variation of MIG welding—Flux-Cored Arc Welding (FCAW): is similar in that it is also a wire-feed process but differs in that it does not require a shielding gas. This gas-free welding application uses Flux-Cored wire to shield the arc, and is a simple, efficient, and effective welding approach, especially when welding outdoors in windy conditions or on dirty materials. The process is widely used in construction because of its high welding speed and portability.

Both MIG and Flux-Cored are very easy to learn and can create extremely clean welds on steel, aluminum, and stainless. Both types have the capability to weld materials as thin as 26 gauge.

TIG Welding/Gas Tungsten Arc Welding (GTAW): TIG welding is an arc welding process that uses a non-consumable tungsten electrode to produce the weld. The weld area is protected from atmospheric contamination by a shielding gas (usually argon), and a filler metal, though some welds, known as autogenous welds, do not require it. A constant-current welding power supply produces energy that is conducted across the arc through a column of highly ionized gas and metal vapors known as plasma.

TIG welding is most commonly used to weld thin sections of alloy steel, stainless steel, and non-ferrous metals such as aluminum, magnesium, and copper alloys. The process grants the operator greater control over the weld than other welding processes, allowing for stronger, higher quality welds. TIG welding is comparatively more complex and difficult to master than other welding types, and is significantly slower.

Below summarizes each welding process. Take a quick glance at what process might be best for your general needs.

Stick Welding

Better suited for windy, outdoor conditions
More forgiving when welding on dirty or rusty metal
Works well on thicker materials

MIG Welding

Easiest process to learn
High welding speeds possible
Better control on thinner metals
Cleaner welds possible with no slag to clean
Same equipment can be used for Flux-Cored Welding

Flux-Cored Welding

Works as well as Stick on dirty or rusty material
Out-of-position welding
Deep penetration for welding thick sections
Increased metal deposition rate
More forgiving when welding on dirty or rusty metal

TIG Welding

Provides highest quality, precise welds
Highly aesthetic weld beads
Allows adjustment of heat input while welding by
use of a foot control

What Process Best Fits Your Needs?

You now have a general overview of the welding processes available, but we still have a ways to go before honing in on the method that will best meet your specific needs.

Let's identify the types of welding projects and materials you will be welding the majority of the time. Will you be creating metal sculptures? Do you intend to restore an old muscle car in your garage? Does the motorcycle you bought years ago require some fabrication? Maybe you intend to do basic repair on equipment used on your farm.

Let's review the following diagram.

Taking this time up front to identify the projects that will occupy the biggest percentage of your welding activity will help you determine the specific thickness of the metal you likely weld most often, and ultimately select the most suitable welder model.

Now let's get a bit more specific. The chart above identifies which weld process you can use for each type of metal. Keep in mind that many of these materials are also processed using varying combinations of two or more metals, a process that is helpful to reinforce strength and functionality.

Metal	Weld Process		
	MIG	Stick	TIG
Steel	•	•	•
Stainless Steel	•	•	•
Aluminum Alloys	•	•	
Cast Iron		•	
Chromoly			•
Copper			•
Brass			•
Exotic metals (Magnesium, Titanium, etc.)			•

Possible Projects	Average Metal Thickness
Auto body	3/16 inch or less
Trailer frames and fencing	1/4 to 5/16 inch
Farm, ranch, and landscape	5/16 to 3/8 inch
Thick structural components	Over 3/8 inch
Bicycles, lawn mowers, or tube frames	1/16 inch
Boats, cars, and motorcycles	1/16 to 1/8 inch
Hunting stands and utility trailers	1/16 to 1/8 inch
General to heavy repair	3/16 to 1/4 inch

What Factors Should you Consider When Determining a Budget?

You likely already have an estimated budget in mind, but first-time owners should consider several important factors when deciding which welder is most appropriate.

The type of welder you purchase should be best suited for the specific functions you require as well as the projects you will be working on the most. Think about your end goal and consider opportunities to expand the usefulness of your welder. In other words, will you need more power and amperage in the future?

In addition to the cost of the welder itself, don't forget to include costs for accessories and supplies you'll need to operate your new welder. This includes welding protection (helmet, gloves, jacket, and so on) as well as gas and consumables.

A Few Last Things to Keep in Mind

We've thrown a lot of information at you in a short amount of time. But now comes the fun part.

On the next page, we'll take a look at some specific welder models offered by Miller in each of the welding process categories developed with the do-it-yourselfer in

❱ Miller's Diversion 180 is the perfect TIG welder for the home hobbyist.

❱ One of the most versatile MIG machines available is the Millermatic 211. It features the revolutionary Auto-Set function that takes the guesswork out of selecting the proper heat range.

❱ Plasma cutters have made cutting torches virtually obsolete. Miller offers a variety of machines ranging in applications from home shops to production facilities

mind. As you review the list of Miller offerings, take note of the varying amperage requirements of each, including power requirements and duty-cycle necessary to achieve the most effective and economical operational results.

So what is duty cycle, you ask? One way of classifying a welder's "size" is by how much amperage it can generate at a given "duty cycle." Duty cycle is the number of minutes out of a 10-minute period a welder can operate. For example, a Dynasty 350 TIG unit can deliver 300 amps of welding output at a 60 percent duty cycle. It can weld continuously at 300 amps for six minutes, and then must cool down during the remaining four minutes to prevent overheating.

To see if a machine meets your do-it-yourselfer needs, consider the following power classifications: Light Industrial products typically have a 20 percent duty cycle and a rated output of 230 amps or lower. More industrial products typically have a 40 to 60 percent duty cycle and a rated output of 300 amps or lower.

The Miller lineup of welders also incorporates several exclusive features, including their Adaptive Hot Start technology, which means you no longer have to worry about those difficult-to-strike stick electrodes. The Multi Voltage Plug (MVP) allows you to connect to common 115V or 230V power receptacles without the use of any tools. Simply choose the plug that fits the receptacle and connect it to the power cord.

Don't feel you have to make a purchasing decision right now. Take some time to define your needs. If you have questions about welding processes, benefits, limitations, or operation, or something is unclear, call Miller. And when you're ready to match a specific model with the task, hobby, or business they will suggest the model or product that is the best for you.

LET'S GO SHOPPING

Stick Welders

To review, the Stick welding process is ideal for general construction, maintenance and repair, shipboard installation/repair, farm and ranch applications, home repair, and plant fabrication/repair. Miller compact designs allow for greater portability. When considering duty cycle for a Stick machine, note that most Stick electrodes are consumed in less than two minutes. About 80 percent of all Stick welding is done with an 1/8-inch-diameter electrode, which takes about one minute to consume.

Suggested Products:
Maxstar 150S
Thunderbolt XL 225/150 AC/DC

MIG/Flux-Cored Welders

Again, the MIG welding process is ideal for general maintenance and repair, farm and ranch applications, home repair, and autobody. Key features exclusive to the Millermatic family of MIG welders include:

Auto-Set: A breakthrough control that automatically sets your welder to the proper parameters. Auto-Set offers all-in-one MIG minus the guesswork. Simply set the wire diameter and material thickness and you're ready to start welding.

Standard Built-In Solid-State Contactor Circuit: Makes wire electrically "cold" until trigger is pulled. This makes the unit safer and torch easier to position before starting to weld.

Thermal Overload Protection: Shuts down the unit and activates over-temperature light if airflow is blocked or duty cycle is exceeded. Automatically resets when fault is corrected and unit cools.

Suggested Products:

Millermatic 140 Auto-Set
Millermatic 180 Auto-Set
Millermatic 211 Auto-Set with MVP
Millermatic Passport Plus
Millermatic 212 Auto-Set
Millermatic 252

TIG Welders

Miller Diversion AC/DC TIG welders contain all the features you need to make welding easy, fun, and affordable. The TIG welding process is ideal for home repair, garage and shop jobs, autobody, chassis/frame fabrication, aluminum oil pans, stainless exhaust, metal art, and sheetmetal applications.

Key features exclusive to Miller include:

Easy-to-Understand Operator Interface

It's as easy as 1, 2, 3 to set your machine and start welding!
1. Power up
2. Select material type
3. Set material thickness range

Inverter Technology

By utilizing an inverter-based AC/DC power source, a more efficient (consumes less energy) and consistent welding arc is provided than older transformer-based machines.

Eliminates Waste of Expensive Shielding Gas

Miller's Auto-Postflow feature optimizes postflow time based on welding amperage. This allows for proper shielding of both the weld end zone and electrode every time without waste of gas or need for adjustment.

❯ *Something that makes welding much easier is the self-darkening helmet—Miller offers a variety of them.*

Reduced Noise, Maintenance, and Operating Costs

Miller's Fan-On-Demand cooling system operates only when needed. This cuts down on fan noise, along with reducing power consumption and contaminants drawn into the machine.

Suggested Products:

Diversion 165
Diversion 180
Dynasty 200 Series

To access a thorough listing of all Miller welder models, supplies, and related accessories, visit millerwelds.com/products. You may also request a free full-line catalog of welding and cutting equipment by visiting the literature request page at millerwelds.com. Here you can also find information on Miller's welding protection and safety apparel, safety guidelines and resources, distributor network, product registration, and other welding resources.

A variety of Miller products were used in the construction of the AMSOIL/*STREET RODDER* '51 Ford including:
Diversion 180
Dynasty 350
Millermatic 211 Auto-Set
Millermatic 252
ArcStation
Two X-Clamps
60 Weld Curtain
Spectrum 375 X-TREME
Spectrum 875
Arc Armor Welding Protection (gloves, helmets, jackets, and so on)

FLAMING RIVER

Simple and Effective
Rack-and-Pinion Steering

Our Ford was originally equipped with what is called worm and roller steering. While it was an improvement over the worm and sector style used earlier, eventually Ford, and the rest of the automotive industry, adopted recirculating ball steering. As the name implies, this type of steering gear uses a series of ball bearings that roll between the gears in the steering box to reduce friction and wear. While this design made steering easier, it also dramatically increased the service life of the steering gear as a result of the increased wear surface supplied by the balls rolling between the friction points.

The next big advancement in steering was the rack-and-pinion. A relatively simple design, a gear on the end of the steering shaft engages the teeth in a long bar called a rack and the ends of the rack are attached to the tie-rod ends. Turning the steering wheel makes the gear revolve, which moves the rack and ultimately the wheels. Rack-and-pinion steering is simple with few moving and pivoting parts, it's also precise and provides the driver with excellent feedback and road feel. But while it has obvious advantages, worm and roller and recirculating ball boxes do offer more mechanical advantage, so in most cases rack-and-pinion was used in lightweight cars while a conventional gearbox was found in heavier vehicles. That was true until power racks came along. Power racks are now found in a number of larger cars. Thanks to the lightweight engine, Honest Charley Garage opted for a manual rack for the AMSOIL/*STREET RODDER* Road Tour '51.

❯ The basics of a rack-and-pinion steering gear: The pinion gear is attached to the steering shaft, the rack converts the rotary motion of the steering wheel to the linear movement required to turn the wheels.

❯ The spool valve mounts to the rack—it controls the fluid from the pump that supplies the power assist to the rack. Like all the other components, Flaming River builds these in-house.

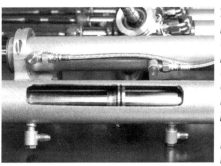

❯ In a power rack, pressurized fluid from the power steering pump is directed by the spool valve into one of the ports on the rack cylinder, which port is determined by which way you are turning. The hydraulic force inside the cylinder then pushes on the piston that is attached to the rack gear. This hydraulic force is what gives the driver the power assist.

Choosing the Right Rack

Flaming River offers rack-and-pinion steering in manual and power designs for front and rear steer applications in a wide variety of configurations, so finding the proper gear for any application isn't a problem.

While there are exceptions, most aftermarket IFS applications that require a front steer rack use a Ford-style gear. There are two versions of this steering, the 1974-78 Mustang II style with 16 inches between mounting points, and the 1979-93 Mustang style with 15-1/2 inches between the mounts. The chassis is designed to either style.

It should be noted that in addition to the variations in mounting dimensions, steering gear travel is also a consideration when selecting a rack—too little travel and the car's turning circle will be larger than necessary; too much travel and there may be interference between the tires and the chassis on hard turns. While light rubbing between the tires and chassis may happen occasionally in extreme circumstances (parallel parking, turning in a driveway, and hitting a bump simultaneously), repeated heavy contact must be avoided, as it can cause serious damage to components. In some cases when a long travel rack is used steering stops will be required.

Flaming River Parts List:

PN FR20006	32-inch Paintable Tilt Column, 2-inch O.D.
PN FR2517DDPl	1DDx3/4 DD SS UJ POL
PN FR2516DDPL	34DDx3/4 DD SS UJ POL
PN FR20114	Factory Drop
PN FR20101	ASM MNT Floor Ring Split ø2.0
PN FR1850-22SSPL	22-inch 3/4-inch DD SS POL Shaft
PN FR1503	1979 Mustang Rack-and-Pinion
PN FR1600	Mounting Bushing
PN FR1601	1974-78 Mustang Outer End

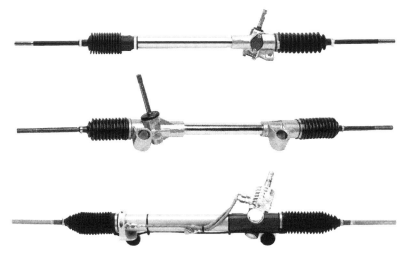

❱ Flaming River builds rack-and-pinion units in a variety of configurations for both front and rear steer applications.

❱ Building a righthand-drive rod? Flaming River can supply a rack-and-pinion gear for that.

❱ With a power rack, the fluid flow (rated in gallons per minute, or gpm) and the line pressure (rated in pounds per square inch, or psi) can also alter how the rack reacts when turning. The higher the gpm and psi the easier or looser the rack may feel. Flaming River calibrates power steering pumps and racks to work together to avoid the oversteer or squirrelly feeling that's commonly found when combining GM pumps with Ford racks.

INSTALLATION TIPS:

Universal Joint Installation

1. Measure and mark 7/8 inch in from the end of the steering shaft
2. Position yoke onto shafting to the 7/8-inch mark. Tighten setscrews to mark shaft
3. Remove yoke
4. Using a 1/4-inch drill bit, countersink the marked position on the shaft
5. Apply red thread locker to threads
6. Reinstall universal joint onto shaft
7. Using a torque wrench, tighten the setscrews to no more than 25 ft-lb
8. Tighten jam nuts
Note: Inspect U-joints frequently to ensure tightness and proper fit

Shaft Installation

Shaft Kit Installation

1) Measure and mark 7/8" in from each end of the DD-style shaft
2) Slide splined u-joint yoke over pinion shaft of rack and pinion
3) Insert DD-style shaft onto opposite end of u-joint
4) Slide DD u-joint over shaft
5) Apply red threadlocker to screws
6) Insert tongue into end of steering column shaft and install through bolt. (Do not tighten the bolt at this time.)
7) Adjust each u-joint to align with the 7/8" mark on the shaft. This ensures proper phasing. Be certain the set screw on the pinion-end yoke shaft is set in the groove in the pinion shaft
8) Snug each set screw (Fig C 1-6) so it will leave a mark on to the DD shaft, to include the tongue
9) Remove shaft kit and dimple (See Fig B) each set screw mark using a ¼" drill bit (Fig C - Set screws 1-6) **WARNING!** Do not dimple the Rack and Pinion shaft; this will cause damage to your rack and pinion which IS NOT covered by warranty.
10) Reassemble shaft kit in car. Tightening each set screw (Fig C Set screws 1-6). Use a torque wrench, tighten each screw to 25 ft-lb. Tighten jam nuts (Fig A) **NOTE:** Periodic inspection of set screws is recommended to ensure that they stay tight.

FAQS

Q: *What different styles of columns does Flaming River offer?*
A: Flaming River offers a variety of Tilt Columns and Non-Tilt Columns available in a wide selection of lengths and sizes. Floor Shift Tilt, Column Shift Tilt, and Tilt Key Columns are our most popular. Key columns can be made in either a Floor Shift or Column Shift style. Our columns come in three finishes: Paintable Mill Finish, Black Powdercoat, and Polished Stainless. Output shafts come in 1 inch to 48 splined shaft, 3/4 inch to 36 splined shaft, and 1 inch DD shaft.

Q: *What is the best way to mount a steering wheel to a Flaming River column?*
A: Flaming River has a wide assortment of Steering Wheel Adapters to fit original or aftermarket steering wheels to our columns. The universal five- and six-bolt wheel adapters contain the pattern for both five- and six-bolt steering wheels, so getting the perfect fit is even easier. Certain steering wheels, like the WaterFall, even have their own adapters to mount to a Flaming River column or original stock column. We also offer three-bolt adapters, nine-bolt adapters, and a number of adapters for Corvette and Mopar applications.

JET-HOT

Jet-Hot explains the technology and science behind header and engine coatings, and the benefits they offer in power and durability.

✳ *BY STEPHEN KIM* ✳ *PHOTOGRAPHY BY THE AUTHOR* ✳

In the walk of the hot rodding aftermarket, the term *battle tested* serves merely as a euphemism for track-tested racing hardware. When the products at hand are Jet-Hot's well-known ceramic coatings, however, that euphemism transforms into a literary truth. Before entering the automotive market, Jet-Hot earned its red, white, and blue stripes developing coatings for the U.S. military. Whether the challenge at hand was providing a thermal barrier on fighter jet engines and submarine parts, or protecting the launch gear on aircraft carriers, Uncle Sam turned to Jet-Hot to get the job done during the heat of combat. Recognizing the benefits of Jet-Hot coatings, the Army began using them on armored vehicles as well.

Eventually, Jet-Hot pondered the benefits of applying its proven coating technology to automotive applications. After extensive research, the company developed coatings specifically for automotive use, and racers and enthusiasts alike quickly realized the benefits of Jet-Hot's ceramic coatings. In the past, header coatings were nothing more than aesthetic products that provided little to no thermal protection, but Jet-Hot changed all that by offering coatings that not only prevented corrosion, but also looked great. In recent years, engine builders have realized the benefits of applying Jet-Hot's thermal coatings on internal components such as pistons and cylinder head combustion chambers. Furthermore, the company has also developed a complete line of antifriction and oil-shedding coatings. To get the full scoop on coating technology, and how hot rodders can use them in their own rides, we sat down and chatted with Jet-Hot's Dave Burton. Here's what he had to say:

Origin of Coatings

Coating technology was first applied to headers in 1981. The technology was an adaptation of similar coatings Jet-Hot developed for the aerospace industry as a means of protecting high-temperature metals from oxidation. The extreme heat created by fighter jet engines, the corrosive environments they operate in, and the countless heat cycles they're subjected to caused very rapid parts wear, so the military turned to Jet-Hot to develop coatings that extended component longevity. Furthermore, Jet-Hot has supplied proprietary coatings to protect the parts on aircraft carrier launch systems for the U.S. Navy, as well as coatings for the U.S. Army's armored vehicles. Leveraging upon years of experience learned from providing long-term protection from corrosion and thermal fatigue in military applications, Jet-Hot transitioned into the automotive aftermarket in the early '90s. These coatings are similar, but have been updated

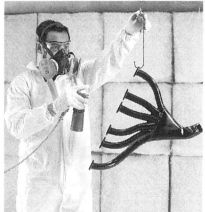

and enhanced over the years to meet the specific needs of the automotive segment. Jet-Hot is constantly developing and testing new coatings for specialized applications and solutions. Customers can rest assured that Jet-Hot uses the same technology in our automotive applications as in our military applications to provide a superior level of protection.

Automotive Transition

Given Jet-Hot's extensive track record in heavy-duty military applications, we began exploring how to apply our coating technology to address the heat management issues in hot rods and race cars. After releasing our first automotive products, Jet-Hot became the number-one coating brand on the market within five years. Enthusiasts also appreciated the high-sheen finish provided by our coatings. In the early '90s, Jet-Hot became the only coating company to support racers at the track. Legendary NHRA Funny Car champion John Force recognized the safety benefits of Jet-Hot coatings early on, as they substantially reduced header temperatures. His crew chiefs discovered that Jet-Hot's coatings allowed for quicker cool down periods, allowing them to rebuild their race motors more quickly between rounds.

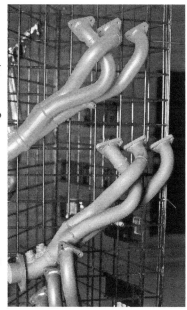

Coating Makeup

Ceramic is a rather generic term that doesn't necessarily describe the makeup of a coating. All coatings are not created equal, and several elements go into Jet-Hot's coating that give it its heat and corrosion resistance properties and distinguishes it from the competition. At a glance people only see the aluminum part of a coating. Ceramics in general are compounds that are inorganic and nonmetallic. Since organic compounds contain carbon that burns under extreme heat, eliminating them from a coating is very important. This is what makes ceramic coatings different from a powdercoat or epoxy, both of which have carbon bonds that start breaking down at 600-800 degrees F. Additionally, ceramics contain binders that hold everything together. A coating's filler material can be a pigment, paint, or aluminum. Using aluminum in our coatings allows polishing it to a high-sheen finish that enthusiasts are familiar with. The end result is a coating that not only offers high-temperature and corrosion resistance, but also looks great.

Coating Process

Jet-Hot's ceramic coatings can be applied to any set of headers, both old and new, and are backed by a lifetime warranty. After receiving the parts at our facility, they are inventoried into our computer and scribed with the order number on the pipes themselves. We also take a photo of every incoming order for referencing purposes. The next

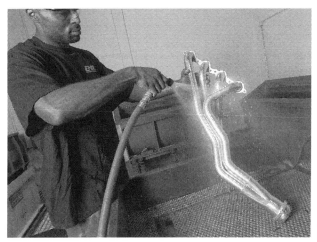

Inside and Out

It's not uncommon to only coat the outside of a header, but at Jet-Hot we feel it's important to coat the inside of the header tubes as well. There are several advantages of doing so, which is why we coat all headers on both the inside and outside. Since water vapor is a combustion by-product, as a motor and exhaust system cools down, water condenses and rusts a header from the inside out. To prevent this, Jet-Hot has developed special fixtures and techniques to apply our coating to the inside surface of header tubing. Regardless of how complex the inside of the tubing may be, we have developed methods to apply coatings to them. Additionally, this yields the benefit of reflecting heat away from the inside surface of the pipes. By reducing the amount of heat transferred through a pipe from the inside out, it keeps the outside header surface cooler as well. Superior heat retention also assists in improving airflow and exhaust scavenging. Furthermore, by ensuring that the heat travels more uniformly across the header surface, it eliminates the potential for heat to build up in localized hot spots. Jet-Hot does not charge extra for this work and provides a full interior coating on all parts. Coupled with a full lifetime warranty, Jet-Hot stands behind its coating and workmanship.

step is cleaning the parts. Usually a thermal degrease or chemical bath works well for light oils, oxides, and other contaminants. Internal engine parts, like pistons, are hand-cleaned with solvents or by using an ultrasonic process. The parts are then grit-blasted to remove scale and debris, and to get the parts down to a clean "white" metal surface. This gives the coating more surface area to grab onto, and ensures good bonding. Once the metal has been cleaned, the ceramic coating is applied using a spray gun similar to those used by body shops. After curing in an oven, the parts may get coated again, if necessary, before they are submerged in a tub of polishing media. The polishing stones vibrate across the metal surface to give the parts a nice sheen, and the parts are then hand-wiped before moving on to final inspection. From start to finish, the coating process takes about two days.

Types of Coatings

Jet-Hot offers several different coating options: Extreme 1300, Extreme 2000, and Extreme 2500. Extreme 1300 is by far our most popular coating. It is easily identified by its polished aluminum finish, and is capable of providing continuous protection to a skin temperature of about 1,300 degrees F. This makes it ideal for naturally aspirated motors, and it can be applied to the majority of parts that we see. The next step up is our Extreme 2000 coating; it contains stainless steel elements that provide thermal protection to skin temperatures of about 2,000 degrees F. This type of coating is best suited for applications with turbos or superchargers that run very hot. Finally, Extreme 2500 is a full ceramic material that provides the best level of insulation for any application. As its name suggests, it can withstand skin temperatures of about 2,500 degrees F. It contains no metal content at all, can only be applied to the outside surfaces of parts, and is often used on components located downstream of turbochargers.

Turbo Applications

Many people are already familiar with the benefits of ceramic header coatings in naturally aspirated engines, but they offer advantages in turbo applications as well. Due to the extreme heat generated by turbo motors, Jet-Hot recommends using our Extreme 2000 or Extreme 2500 coatings in turbo applications. Coating the hot side parts can maintain the heat inside components better for improved thermal efficiency. Furthermore, our coatings help spread the heat out more uniformly. Interestingly, in rear-mount turbo combinations customers have reported reduced turbo lag when using Jet-Hot coatings.

Coating Maintenance

One of the biggest benefits of a coated header is its shiny good looks, but as the miles and years tack on, regular maintenance is required to prevent dulling and staining. Jet-Hot recommends that customers periodically clean their headers to remove any salt or road grime that can accumulate on the surface. The best way to do this is with light soap and cool water. Oil, transmission fluid, and engine coolant can be easily removed with fine steel wool or a Scotch-Brite pad. Any nonabrasive polish can then be used with a soft cloth to bring out a high-luster finish.

Aluminum will cloud up when cleaned in a hot condition, so it's imperative to allow the surface to cool down first. If headers are dulling, the coating is getting too hot for the application, or there is residue that's causing the color change. Furthermore, uneven fuel distribution and improper spark timing can result in extreme exhaust gas temperature that may exceed the temperature range of a coating. To avoid this, it's important to make sure an engine is in optimal running condition. Jet-Hot customers can also rest assured that their header coatings are covered by a lifetime warranty. If there's ever a problem, just ship the headers in and we'll re-coat them under warranty.

Internal Thermal Coatings

With racing classes as competitive as they are these days, engine builders are increasingly using coatings on internal engine components to search for extra horsepower. In addition to exhaust coatings, Jet-Hot also offers coatings for internal engine components such as pistons, crankshafts, and bearings. Internal engine coatings fall

into three categories: ceramic metallic thermal coatings, friction reduction coatings, and oil-shedding coatings. Ceramic coatings are often applied to piston crowns, valve faces, and the cylinder head combustion chambers. This provides thermal management and helps retain heat in the combustion chamber for improved power.

Antifriction Coatings

Friction reduction coatings provide improved lubrication and cooling to extend the life of internal engine components. On bearings and piston skirts, fluoropolymer coatings are designed to help maintain the oil film on the surface. The benefit is reduced friction, improved longevity, and increased horsepower. The coatings are very effective, yet thin enough that they don't impact bearing or piston-to-wall clearances at all. While the purpose of ceramic coatings on the valve faces is to maintain heat in the combustion chamber, an antifriction coating can also be applied to the valve stem. The resulting friction reduction can help prevent engine damage caused by sticking a valve.

Oil-Shedding Coatings

Engine oil not only lubricates parts, but it also carries heat away from internal components. Oil-shedding coatings allow oil to perform its job by carrying that heat away more efficiently. As such, oil-shedding coatings are typically applied to valvesprings, and the inside surfaces of valve covers and oil pans. The more oil these components can shed, the more heat that can be carried away. Other favorable characteristics of these coatings are that they're highly resistant to chemical acids and bases, and improve oil drain-back and oil management.

Cooler Air Temps

Keeping the temperature of the intake air charge as cool as possible results in a denser air/fuel charge, which increases horsepower. A cooler air intake charge is also more resistant to detonation. While it's true that header coatings reduce underhood temperature, and therefore the heat that soaks into neighboring components, the intake manifold itself can also be coated. Applying a ceramic coating on the bottom surface of the intake manifold mitigates the amount of heat that will transfer from the hot engine and engine oil into the intake runners. This keeps both the air and fuel cooler. The inside of the intake runners can also be coated, which sometimes improves the laminar flow characteristics of the induction system. In the near future, Jet-Hot plans on conducting extensive dyno testing in-house to measure the performance benefits of our engine coatings.

Coatings and Welding

Since there are often clearance issues with headers, they sometimes need to be cut, welded, or modified for proper fitment. For the sake of simplicity, it is always best to complete these modifications or repairs before sending a set of headers in to get coated. This eliminates the possibility of having a section of tubing where the coating is no longer present. In the event that a section of tubing that has already been coated needs to be welded, the coating must be removed with a grinder. Likewise, the heat of the weld must be increased as well.

Coatings and Dynos

When driving down the road, there is always a steady stream of air that removes heat from the engine compartment. However, this isn't the case on an engine or chassis dyno. The stagnant air in a dyno cell combined with the heat generated by sustained high-rpm engine operation can exceed the limitations of the aluminum in the coating matrix. This can ultimately cause dulling of the coating surface. To avoid this potential problem, it's best to use a large fan to help dissipate the heat of the engine and headers during dyno testing.

SOFFSEAL

It never fails. You may think your hot rod is complete but there's always "just one more thing." Road Tour chauffeur Jerry Dixey was sniveling that rain was coming in through the door gaps. Turns out in the rush to get the car on the road we had forgotten to install the rubber door molding from SoffSeal. (Since we had chopped the top the rain gutters were smoothed over.) Coming to our rescue was Jeff Hubert of SoffSeal who walked over from his booth at the 2013 Street Rod Nats with a roll of rubber door seal. While ol' Editor Brennan looked on but not much in the way of help, Hubert was able to place rubber weatherstripping on both doors. This should make Dixey a lot happier in the rain!

❯ Editor Brennan (left) and Jeff Hubert of SoffSeal (right) working on laying down weatherstripping.

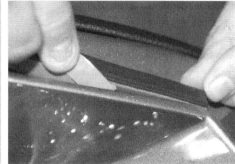

❯ Once you've pressed the rubber against the metal then you can begin to peel back another couple of inches of the adhesive covering.

❯ Start with a clean edge and peel back only enough tape to give you enough exposed rubber to start the project. (Resist temptation to take off all of the adhesive covering.)

❯ Be patient and go along the area to be covered slowly.

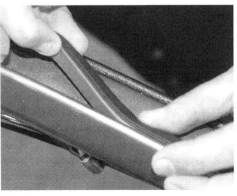

❯ Moving along in several-inch increments, press the SoffSeal rubber firmly against the surface. (Make sure the surface is clean; you may want to use rubbing alcohol to clean the metal surface.)

❯ In the beginning you might want to map out your area to be covered and cut to fit. Don't "stretch" the rubber as you lay out the area to be covered.

WHEEL VINTIQUES

Wheel Vintiques is proud to be the leading supplier of OEM reproduction and custom steel wheels. Established in 1986, Wheel Vintiques offers an enormous product line of wheels, accessories, and more. With products to fit hot rods and customs, restored classics, and trucks, Wheel Vintiques caters to collector car enthusiasts of all genres.

All Wheel Vintiques products are made from high-quality steel, and they're manufactured right here in the United States. With the utmost attention to detail and quality, Wheel Vintiques products are built to last, with many options for show-quality chrome plating, painting, and powdercoating. Rigorous testing and heightened quality control ensures customer satisfaction, while improved customer service will keep you coming back. Wheel Vintiques stocks every item within its massive warehouse in City of Industry, California, so order turnaround and delivery is a quick and painless process.

From OEM wheel reproductions to custom-sized wheels for hot rods and muscle cars, Wheel Vintiques is your steel and wire wheel headquarters.

IDENTIFYING WHEEL DIMENSIONS

There are four important measurements that are used to categorize and identify a wheel for fitment purpose. They are:

A. RIM DIAMETER
This is the actual diameter of the wheel at the point where the tire bead seats (not the outer lip).

B. RIM WIDTH
Measure this from the inside of the outer lip at the bead seating point to the inner lip.

C. BACK SPACING
A very important measurement is from the inside of the wheel at the point where it contacts the hub, brake drum or axle flange to the inside edge (lip) of the wheel.

D. BOLT PATTERN
Count the number of mounting holes for the wheel and determine the diameter of a circle that would run through their center. On a 4, 6 or 8-lug wheel it's a direct measurement. On a 5-lug wheel, you can measure from the center of one hole to the OUTER edge of the hole diagonally across from it and get an approximate number that's very close to the bolt circle diameter.

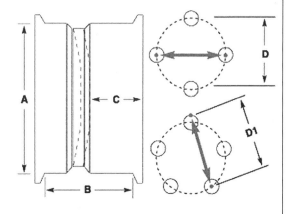

DETERMINE PROPER FITMENT

VEHICLE CLEARANCE
In many instances, the objective will be to fit a larger tire within the confines of a given wheel well or fender. To make sure there is ample clearance for the tire and wheel (including considerations for suspension travel and brake drums/calipers), a number of measurements must be taken and supplied to the Wheel Vintiques tech staff. Please refer to the drawing to the right for reference.

A__ D__
B__ E__
C__ F__

DISC BRAKES
The brand/model (aftermarket) or year/make/model of OEM discs, or the following dimensions will be required to provide necessary clearance for brake calipers:

A__
B__
C__
D__
E__

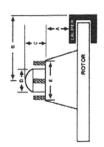

DRUM BRAKES
The year/make/model of OEM drum brakes or following dimensions are required to assure proper fitment:

A__
B__
C__
D__
E__

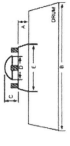

DAKOTA DIGITAL

Known for manufacturing state-of-the-art digital instrumentation in vehicle-specific and universal clusters, as well as individual units, Dakota Digital also offers the VHX series that combines analog and digital instrumentation in one package.

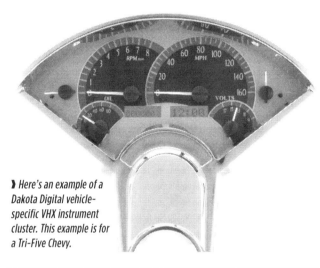

❯ Here's an example of a Dakota Digital vehicle-specific VHX instrument cluster. This example is for a Tri-Five Chevy.

❯ The high-tech innards of a VHX instrument—don't worry, we don't recognize anything either, but we know they work great.

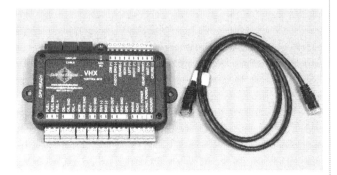

❯ This is the VHX control box that allows the senders to communicate to the instruments.

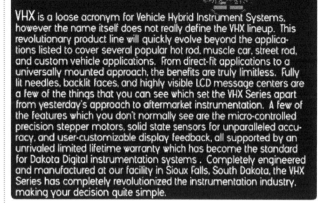

What is VHX?

VHX is a loose acronym for Vehicle Hybrid Instrument Systems, however the name itself does not really define the VHX lineup. This revolutionary product line will quickly evolve beyond the applications listed to cover several popular hot rod, muscle car, street rod, and custom vehicle applications. From direct-fit applications to a universally mounted approach, the benefits are truly limitless. Fully lit needles, backlit faces, and highly visible LCD message centers are a few of the things that you can see which set the VHX Series apart from yesterday's approach to aftermarket instrumentation. A few of the features which you don't normally see are the micro-controlled precision stepper motors, solid state sensors for unparalleled accuracy, and user-customizable display feedback, all supported by an unrivaled limited lifetime warranty which has become the standard for Dakota Digital instrumentation systems . Completely engineered and manufactured at our facility in Sioux Falls, South Dakota, the VHX Series has completely revolutionized the instrumentation industry, making your decision quite simple.

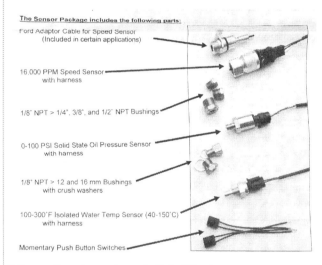

The Sensor Package includes the following parts:

Ford Adaptor Cable for Speed Sensor (Included in certain applications)

16,000 PPM Speed Sensor with harness

1/8" NPT > 1/4", 3/8", and 1/2" NPT Bushings

0-100 PSI Solid State Oil Pressure Sensor with harness

1/8" NPT > 12 and 16 mm Bushings with crush washers

100-300°F Isolated Water Temp Sensor (40-150°C) with harness

Momentary Push Button Switches

❯ These are the various senders used with the VHX series gauges.

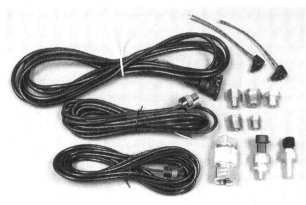

❯ Wiring for the instruments and control box are simple plug-and-play.

The '51 Ford Road Tour Custom Combines Plenty of Old-Time Kool with Today's Technology

✳ BY BRIAN BRENNAN ✳ PHOTOGRAPHY BY ROBERT MCGAFFIN ✳

Each year we embark on a magazine build, and before you is our latest Road Tour effort. A build that was a first—being a true custom—for the long succession of Road Tour cars, we present you with this year's '51 Ford (oftentimes called a "shoebox").

But where do we start? OK, let's answer the two most commonly asked questions: "What color is it?" and "What is the wheel and tire combination?" The color is straight from a PPG can called Golden Dream (PN 908324) and it originates from within their Vibrance Collection. As for the rolling stock it is comprised of a set of Wheel Vintiques smoothies and Coker American Classic whitewalls.

A little on the history of the car: Tucked in a corner of Fatman Fabrications' shop, Brent Vandervort pointed out a well-driven '51 Ford. After the obligatory, "I will trade you several of these, four of those, and I might throw in that over there for your decent-looking '51 Tudor sedan," a deal was struck for our soon-to-be 2013 AMSOIL/*STREET RODDER* Road Tour car. (The Tudor sedan has the longer roof than the more commonly used Business Coupe.)

Since we were wandering around Fatman we thought we would do a bit more "shopping" and pick up a '49-51 Ford chassis complete with stainless steel IFS control arms, front and rear sway bars, a Flaming River manual rack-and-pinion, QA1 Proma Star adjustable shocks, Wilwood disc brakes (11-inch rotors in front and 10-3/4-inch rotors in back), a Dynotech driveshaft linked to a Ford 9-inch fitted with 4.11 gears and a limited-slip differential. The Fatman chassis is based on 3/16-inch wall rectangular 1020 SAE steel tubing that measures 2x5 inches

❯ The frenched headlights come by way of Yogi's, while the grille opening is custom by the HCG staff. The opening houses the U.S. Radiator triple-flow copper and brass radiator, the Vintage Air condenser, and the HCG fabricated intercooler. The stock bumper was narrowed and smoothed over while the custom grille surround was plated at Sherm's Custom Plating who did all of the car's brightwork.

and is all neatly welded together via Miller Electric Manufacturing Company equipment. The frame was modified using a newly relocated rear crossmember so that the body would clear the tapered channel job. (Did you notice the top chop, 2 inches in front and 3-1/2 inches in back, and that the car is channeled?) Resting at the corners are the ever-popular Coker American Classic 235R55-17 radial rubber sporting 1-3/4-inch whitewalls mounted to 17x7 Wheel Vintiques smoothies, each with 5-1/2-inch backspacing and 5-on-4.5 bolt patterns.

We've always wanted to work with the staff at Honest Charley Garage (think Coker Tire) and here was a project that was both geographically and mechanically desirable. Turns out our intuition was right on. A quick phone call to Intercity Lines, our go-to guys for moving projects around the country, and the once Fatman soon-to-be Road Tour shoebox was on its way to Honest Charley Garage (HCG).

Under the watchful eye of Greg Cunningham the staff at HCG was off and building—once all concerned could agree on which version of the Eric Black–inspired concept drawings would be "the one." Now is a good time to mention that we had given the craftsmen at HCG plenty of time to

complete the task at hand—10 months. (Hey, if TV stars can build a car in seven days, having 10 months should be a piece of cake!) Oh, did we mention that instead of a nifty '51 we wanted a full custom? Still 10 months, come on, how hard can it be?

If you have followed along on the pages of *STREET RODDER* this past year you know just how much effort was put forth repairing rusted sheetmetal (and that's an understatement!) and how much custom metalwork was performed as well as all of the other finer points that turned this into a righteous-looking custom. The guys at HCG used just about every patch panel offered by Dennis Carpenter Ford Restoration Parts and a few that only HCG could fabricate. Now would also be a good time to mention that our shoebox is powered by the latest from Ford Racing Performance: the EcoBoost 3.5L twin-turbo V-6 and a Ford 6R80 automatic overdrive. Other engine accessories include the custom exhaust system built

at HCG and using Flowmaster exhaust pipe and DBX mufflers. Flowmaster was also involved in assisting HCG in making the ducting required for the twin-turbo inlet tubing. All of the exhaust system was then coated by Jet-Hot in one of their high-performance coatings.

While at the SEMA Show this past year we literally rolled the motor out of the Ford booth and into the HCG trailer and the motor was on its way. Of course, no one on our end had any knowledge on how to make this engine and trans package work in a hot rod. Ford Racing provided what they could but the real head scratching, hair pulling, and good ol' gnashing of teeth befell the engineers at FAST (Fuel Air Spark Technology).

We "leaned" on FAST for their expertise on EFI and engine management systems for modern Detroit motors. Our first stop was David Page of FAST who turned us over to two FAST engineers, Ron Wiggins and Lance Ward. It was up to them to design the "tuning package" that would

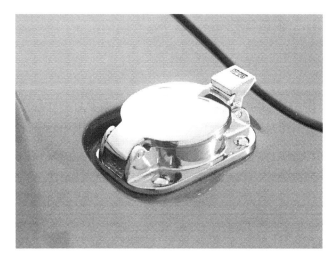

allow the use of a FAST XFI 2.0 and their wiring harness to match up to the Painless Performance Products chassis harness and make this hot rod run.

Of course, there was one more bit of significant electronics to overcome and that was the Ford trans package. The Ford 6R80 had to work with the EcoBoost and the rest of the car's electronics and for this we did some more leaning—this time it was on Jay Rohrback of PCS. As it turns out PCS has a controller available so making our 6R80 function was less of a problem than we had anticipated. Turns out our tranny originally hailed from a '12 Ford F-150 mounted behind an EcoBoost. Rohrback took the lead and came up with the necessary controller to make it shift via a Lokar-mounted floor shifter and the paddle shifters on the modified steering wheel fitted with a stock '51 Ford horn emblem.

We mentioned earlier that the shoebox had undergone a plethora of metalwork. One only has to look at earlier issues of *SR* to get a good inkling of just how much. With several drawers full of Eastwood bodyworking tools, Miller welding equipment, Dennis Carpenter Ford Restoration Parts patch panels, boxes full of PPG paint materials, the build was on in earnest to get the car ready for our beloved mullet-adorned chauffeur, Jerry Dixey, to have in time to make each of his appointed summertime rounds. Eventually this equated to nearly 23,000 miles in roughly 12 weeks. Dixey tells us that the '51 approaches 400 miles on the just-over 16-gallon Rock Valley Antique Auto Parts gas tank, equipped with a complete Aeromotive fuel delivery system that includes pump, filter, lines, and necessary hardware. (Dixey also tells us that he personally can go 250 miles. *Editor's note: Not sure what he means but we believe he's bragging.*) We also made sure that the trunk was filled with plenty of Golden Shine car detail products. (We figured Dixey would have it so easy cruising in the AMSOIL/*STREET RODDER* '51 custom that we

❯ *There's a great deal of custom work on the interior; note the dash, center console, door panels, seating, and even the steering wheel with an original '51 emblem/horn button.*

wanted to make sure he had something to do at the end of each day!)

Although the top chop is obvious, albeit a mild chop, the car does feature a tapered channel effort from front to back. It isn't surprising that one might miss the channel given the pancaked hood, smooth quarter-panels, reworked dashboard, the deleted gas filler (the Rock Valley stainless steel tank is trunk mounted), the chromed (by way of Sherm's Custom Chrome Plating who also handled all of the brightwork) custom side molding, frenched headlights, and custom taillights from Lokar Performance as well as a totally rethought and reshaped grille opening. The grille needed to be reworked to house the HCG fabricated intercooler, a Vintage Air condenser, and U.S. Radiator brass and copper radiator complete a shrouded electric fan would now fill the opening. Look closely and you will see that the front and rear bumpers are stock in

origin but both narrowed and smoothed. All of this nifty metalwork came straight from the workbenches within HCG. After the "heavy lifting" the body and paintwork was handled at HCG bringing to life the PPG Golden Dream gold tones making this year's Road Tour car a striking looking custom.

Inside the '51 is very spacious, space normally at a premium in a street rod. The Wise Guys buckets are stitched in black vinyl coupled with N.O.S. '58 Buick cloth in a black and gray combo; again the handiwork came from the sewing machine at HCG. In back the custom runs sans seating but it is nonetheless neatly finished in matching black leather and stitched in red are the Wise Guys buckets. Other interior trim such as the door and kick panels, custom center console, headliner, and carpeting are more top-of-the-line effort from HCG.

Making sure that chauffeur Dixey maintains the

❯ The sedan features Wise Guys custom-upholstered bucket seats that sport red stitching over the black vinyl surrounding the center panels made from N.O.S. '58 Buick cloth in a black and white coloring. The three-point belts are another Wise Guys touch.

❯ Visible is the Flaming River steering column, topped with an original-style wheel neatly "hiding" the paddle shifters from Powertrain Control Solutions. The custom center console that houses the Lokar shifter is another piece of custom work from the workbenches at HCG. Aside from housing the shifter it's also home for the stereo.

lifestyle he has grown accustomed to, creature comforts abound in the light of a Vintage Air cooling and heat system, Dakota Digital instrumentation, and plenty of Dynamat nestled under the custom carpet work to keep out unwanted sounds and heat. Keeping more unwanted outside climes and sound falls to the door glass operated by Specialty Power Windows (who also did the windshield wipers) mechanisms and SoffSeal, which provided all of the rubber used throughout the build. We wouldn't want Dixey to become taxed so a Lokar shifter is mounted center within the custom console and in case he tires there's a PCS paddle shifter resting behind the modified steering wheel. The pedal assembly is more Lokar touches

as are the interior door and window handles. If you look closely you will see there are two dash-mounted clocks. One is a traditional Dakota Digital analog timepiece while the other is a highly accurate battery-powered sweep-hand rally clock, as would be used in the Great Race, with a custom face presented to HCG for use within the '51 again by Dakota Digital. One can't help but notice all of the dash touches, including the custom-face Dakota Digital gauge cluster based on a stock-appearing gauge cluster that features a single-face gauge (custom background) but is outfitted with speedo, tach, fuel, volt, oil, and water temp. The dash also houses the Vintage Air outlets and controls. The entire behind-the-

scenes wiring is cleanly handled by a Painless Performance Products 18-circuit fuse panel with related wiring, all put into place by HCG craftsmen. And as with any build there are always a myriad of parts and pieces that magically appear, and for that we have to thank Yogi's who supplied all of those "Oh, I thought you had that" hardware.

❱ The rear of the interior is run sans seating but is neatly finished in the same materials as the front. All the upholstery work was performed in-house at HCG. (Chauffeur Dixey is always complaining he doesn't have enough room for his hair and makeup products. Well, here you go!).

❱ Dakota Digital analog gauges are used. Here the stock-appearing single pod is outfitted with a speedo, tach, volt, gas, water temp, and oil pressure gauges. Keyless starter push button is shown below.

❱ Neatly packaged into the corners of the wildly reconfigured '51 dash are the air-conditioning ducts from Vintage Air. Resting below is the headlight switch, which is part of the Painless Performance Products system. You can also see the custom dashpad and trim work aptly handled by HCG.

❱ The custom face rally clock is an HCG touch. It's battery powered and highly accurate. This is the clock that is used to monitor minutes and seconds between stages in timed rallies. (HCG and Coker Tire are huge supporters of the Great Race, a timed rally across America.)

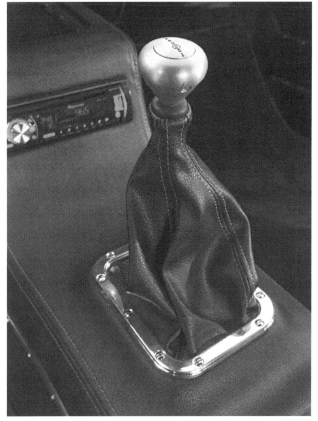

❯ *The Lokar floor shifter (with its own trim ring) is but one means of shifting the Ford automatic overdrive; the other is the PCS paddle shifter mounted behind the steering wheel. The brake and throttle pedals come by way of Lokar.*

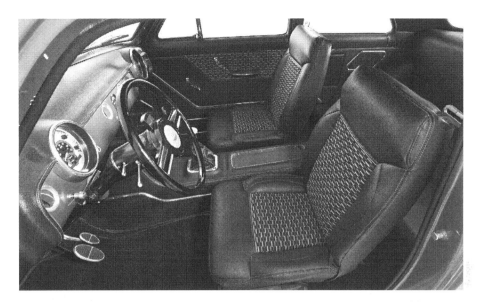

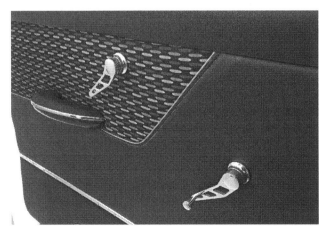

❯ More Lokar appointments include the window crank and door handle neatly mounted to the custom HCG door panels. Note the use of the OEM '58 Buick cloth surrounded by the black Naugahyde.

❯ The trunk is spacious, and this includes the location for the Rock Valley custom-made stainless steel gas tank that houses just over 16 gallons of gas for our 25-mpg Ford Racing EcoBoost twin-turbo 3.5L V-6. Also housed in the trunk is the battery connected via a Painless Performance Products battery install kit.

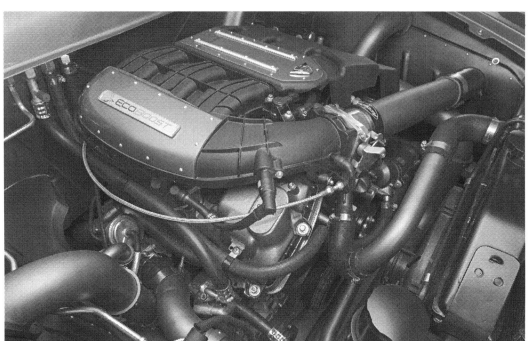

❱ The EcoBoost V-6 was detailed and features custom touches by HCG. Note the throttle cable (no drive-by-wire) comes by way of Lokar. The real effort goes to FAST for coming up with the programming, allowing this engine to be managed by an XFI 2.0 engine management system.

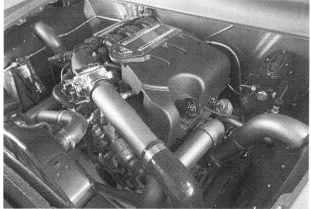

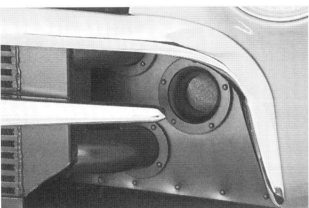

▶ Look closely and you can see one of the two air inlets for the twin turbos that power up the Ford Racing 3.5L EcoBoost V-6. A U.S. Radiator triple-flow radiator is pictured along with the Vintage Air condenser, all packaged where at one time rested a stock Ford cooler.

▶ Coker American Classic narrow whitewall radial rubber is mounted to the Wheel Vintique smoothies. Tire sizing at the corners is 235R55-17 with 1-3/4-inch whitewalls mounted to 17x7 wheels each with 5.5-inch backspacing and 5-on-4.5 bolt patterns. To top matters off, how about a set of spider caps.

▶ Wilwood braking components are used throughout, such as the visible master cylinder and proportioning valve.

▶ Wilwood drilled-and-slotted rotors and aluminum hubs are used at the corners; 11-inch in front and 10-3/4-inch in back. Black powdercoating is featured on the Wilwood Dynalite four-puck calipers. Hiding behind the brakes are the QA1 adjustable coilover shocks used all the way around.

Sponsor Information

Aeromotive Inc.
Fuel System
(913) 647-7300
aeromotiveinc.com

AMSOIL INC.
Lubricants & Filtration
(715) 392-7101
amsoil.com

Coker Tire
Tires
(866) 922-3892
cokertire.com

Dakota Digital
Gauges
(800) 852-3228
dakotadigital.com

**Dennis Carpenter Ford
Restoration Parts**
Body
(704) 786-8139
dennis-carpenter.com

Dynamat
Insulation & Noise Control
(513) 860-5094
dynamat.com

Dynotech
Driveshaft
(800) 633-5559
dynotecheng.com

Eastwood Company
Tools
(800) 345-1178
eastwood.com

FAST
Engine Management
(877) 334-8355
fuelairspark.com

Fatman Fabrications
Chassis & Front Suspension
(704) 545-0369
fatmanfab.com

Flaming River
Steering Components
(866) 815-3669
flamingriver.com

Flowmaster
Exhaust System
(707) 544-4761
flowmastermufflers.com

Ford Racing
Engine
(800) FORD-786
fordracing.com

Golden Shine
Car Care Products
(800) 423-5525
calcarcover.com

Honest Charley Garage
Builder
(877) 295-2045
honestcharley.com

Intercity Lines
Vehicle Transport
(800) 221-3936
intercitylines.com

Jet-Hot
Thermal Coatings
(800) 432-3379
jet-hot.com

Lokar Inc.
Shifter & Accessories
(865) 966-2269
lokar.com

Shifter & Accessories

Welding & Cutting Products

Wiring & Electrical Syetem

Transmission Controller

Paint & Coatings

Shocks, Coils &
Ball Joints

Fuel Tank

Chrome Plating

Weatherstrip

Power
Windows
& Windshield
Wipers

Radiator - Cooling

Air Conditioning

Wheels

Brakes

Seats

Retail Store

Miller Electric Mfg. Co.
Welding & Cutting Products
(800) 426-4553
millerwelds.com

**Painless Performance
Products**
Wiring & Electrical System
(800) 423-9696
painlessperformance.com

Powertrain Control Solutions
Transmission Controller
(804) 227-3023
powertraincontrolsolutions.com

PPG Industries
Paint & Coatings
(440) 572-2800
www.ppg.com/coatings/refinish

QA1
Shocks, Coils & Ball Joints
(800) 721-7761
qa1.net

**Rock Valley
Antique Auto Parts**
Fuel Tank
(800) 344-1934
rockvalleyantiqueautoparts.com

Sherm's Custom Plating
Chrome Plating
(916) 646-0160
shermsplating.com

SoffSeal Inc.
Weatherstrip
(513) 367-0028
soffseal.com

Specialty Power Windows
Power Windows & Wipers
(478) 994-9248
spwkits.com

U.S. Radiator
Radiator & Cooling
(323) 826-0965
usradiator.com

Vintage Air Inc.
Air Conditioning
(800) 862-6658
vintageair.com

Wheel Vintiques
Wheels
(559) 251-6957
wheelvintiques.com

Wilwood Engineering
Brakes
(805) 388-1188
www.wilwood.com

Wise Guys Inc.
Seats
(866) 494-7348
wiseguys-seats.com

Yogi's Inc.
Retail Store
(800) 373-1973
yogisinc.com

Made in the USA
Charleston, SC
31 May 2014